Knits Extraordinaire

President and Chief Executive Officer: Rick Barton
Vice President of Sales: Mike Behar
Director of Finance and Administration: Laticia Mull Dittrich
National Sales Director: Martha Adams
Creative Services: Chaska Lucas
Information Technology Director: Hermine Linz
Controller: Francis Caple
Vice President, Operations: Jim Dittrich
Retail Customer Service Manager: Stan Raynor
Print Production Manager: Fred F. Pruss
Editor-in-Chief: Susan White Sullivan
Director of Designer Relations: Cheryl Johnson
Special Projects Director: Susan Frantz Wiles
Art Publications Director: Rhonda Shelby
Senior Prepress Director: Mark Hawkins

Produced for Leisure Arts, Inc. by Penn Publishing Ltd.
www.penn.co.il
Editor-in-Chief: Rachel Penn
Editor: Shoshana Brickman
Technical editor: Tamara Bostwick
Design and layout: Ariane Rybski
Photography: Roee Fainburg
Styling: Luise Bracha
Make up: Sigal Asraf
Hairstyling: Guy Samuel

PRINTED IN CHINA

ISBN-13: 978-1-60900-144-5
Library of Congress Control Number: 2011930544

Cover photography by Roee Fainburg

Knits Extraordinaire

by

LENA MAIKON

A LEISURE ARTS PUBLICATION

Contents

Introduction

Vintage-style skirts and button-fly short shorts, a matching fingerless glove and shoulder cowl set—these are just some of the high fashion knit patterns you'll find in **Knits Extraordinaire**, the latest book from knitting whiz, Lena Maikon. All of the patterns are fun to make and a pleasure to wear. They take knitting to new levels of style, using traditional techniques, earthy materials and simple shapes.

Many of the garments are made with eco-friendly materials, such as natural wool, bamboo and recycled cotton. These garments reflect a modern sense of style and eco-sensitivity all at the same time. You'll feel great making them and wearing them. Of course, hand-knit items also make fantastic gifts for really good friends!

The projects come in a wide spectrum of colors, ranging from misty grays and greens to bright reds and bold blues. The shapes of the garments are simple, smooth and flattering, and leave plenty of room for self-expression. You'll delight in dressing them up with stunning stockings or extra-wide belts for an even more personal effect.

In several projects, knitting techniques are used to create fabric-like effects, so while the shapes are simple, the textures and designs are interesting. You'll also notice that very few designs require sewn seams. This enables you to create clean, professional-looking garments with ease. No dangling strings or loosely sewn connections! In several garments, you'll find delicate crocheted enhancements to create an even prettier look.

About the Author

Lena Maikon learned to knit and crochet from her grandmother at the age of five in her hometown of Novosibrisk, Russia. She picked up the hobby again many years later, as a form of creative therapy. This quickly turned into a passion and profession. Lena often uses unconventional materials in her designs and dreams of creating a knitted and crocheted world. She crafts socks, shoes, dresses, handbags, flowers, vases, and light fixtures, using not-so-traditional techniques. Lena has published four creative knitting and crocheting books and has her own handmade clothing and accessory label, Leninka. Lena is the mother of two young sons.

Essentials

Standard yarn weight system

Yarn Weight Symbol & Names	LACE 0	SUPER FINE 1	FINE 2	LIGHT 3	MEDIUM 4	BULKY 5	SUPER BULKY 6
Type of Yarns in Category	Fingering, size 10 crochet thread	Sock, Fingering, Baby	DK, Light Worsted	DK, Light Worsted	Worsted, Afghan, Aran	Chunky, Craft, Rug	Bulky, Roving

*GUIDELINES ONLY: The chart above reflects the most commonly used gauges and needle sizes for specific yarn categories.

** Lace weight yarns are usually knitted on larger needles to create lacy openwork patterns. Accordingly, a gauge range is difficult to determine. Always follow the gauge stated in your pattern.

CROCHET TERMINOLOGY

United States	International
slip stitch (slip st)	single crochet (sc)
single crochet (sc)	double crochet (dc)
skip	miss

KNIT TERMINOLOGY

United States	International
gauge	tension
bind off	cast off
yarn over (YO)	yarn forward (yfwd) or yarn around needle (yrn)

SKILL LEVELS

Beginner	Projects for first-time knitters using basic knit and purl stitches. Minimal shaping.
Easy	Projects using basic stitches, repetitive stitch patterns, simple color changes, and simple shaping and finishing.
Intermediate	Projects with a variety of stitches, such as basic cables and lace, simple intarsia, doublepointed needles and knitting in the round needle techniques, mid-level shaping and finishing.
Experienced	Projects using advanced techniques and stitches, such as short rows, fair isle, more intricate intarsia, cables, lace patterns, and numerous color changes.

KNITTING NEEDLES																
U.S.	0	1	2	3	4	5	6	7	8	9	10	10½	11	13	15	17
U.K.	13	12	11	10	9	8	7	6	5	4	3	2	1	00	000	---
METRIC - MM	2	2.25	2.75	3.25	3.5	3.75	4	4.5	5	5.5	6	6.5	8	9	10	12.75

CROCHET HOOKS													
U.S.	B-0	C-2	D-3	E-4	F-5	G-6	H-7	I-9	J-10	K-10½	N	P	Q
METRIC - MM	2.25	2.75	3.25	3.5	3.75	4	5	5.5	6	6.5	9	10	15

Materials and Tools

YARN SELECTION

To make an exact replica of the photographed items, use the yarns listed in the Materials and Tools section of the projects. All of the yarns used in these projects are readily available in the United States and Canada at time of printing.

http://www.stitchnationyarn.com/

http://www.bernat.com/

http://www.redheart.com/

http://www.berroco.com/

http://www.cascadeyarns.com/

http://www.lionbrand.com/

REQUIRED TOOLS AND MATERIALS

For all the projects in this book, you'll need basic items including yarn, knitting needles, scissors and a tape measure. Some projects are knit using standard single-pointed knitting needles; others use circular needles or cable needles. Several projects include crocheted finishing or enhancements that are made using a single crochet hook. Many projects use more than one set of needles.

In some projects, you'll need stitch holders to hold stitches while you are working other stitches; in others, you'll need stitch markers to mark stitches while you work. There are many projects that are knit in one piece so they don't require sewing, but in a few, you will need a yarn needle to sew seams. In such cases, make sure the eye of the needle is wide enough for threading the yarn. You may also need a sewing needle and thread to sew on buttons.

To make pompoms for the Fabulously Flared Pompom Skirt (page 76), you'll need tracing paper, a pencil, and a permanent marker for copying the templates and transferring them to leather or cardboard. Buttons, elastic thread, and jute twine rope are used to fasten various garments.

Most importantly, make sure you have everything you need before starting each project and always read the instructions from start to finish before starting.

TABLE OF WOMEN'S SIZES						
5'5"-5'6"/165cm-168cm tall, average bust, average back						
U.S./Europe	6/36	8/38	10/40	12/42	14/44	16/46
Bust	33"/84cm	35"/88cm	36"/92cm	38"/96cm	39½"/100cm	41"/104cm
Waist	26½"/66cm	27½"/70cm	29"/74cm	30¾"/78cm	32¼"/82cm	34"/86cm
Hips	35.5"/90cm	37"/94cm	38½"/98cm	40"/102cm	41¾"/106cm	43"/110cm
Back Waist Length	16½"/41cm	16½"/41cm	16½"/41cm	16½"/41cm	16½"/41cm	16½"/41cm
Shoulder Width	4¾"/12cm	4¾"/12cm	5"/13cm	5"/13cm	5"/13cm	5"/13cm
Sleeve Length	23½"/60cm	23½"/60cm	23½"/60cm	23½"/60cm	23½"/60cm	23½"/60cm
Upper Arm	10½"/27cm	11"/28cm	11½"/29cm	12"/30cm	12¼"/31cm	12½"/32cm

Basic

◇◇◇◇◇◇◇

SIZE

At the beginning of each pattern, you'll find the sizes in which the pattern can be knit and the size in which the pattern was photographed. For example: 36/38 (40/42, 44/46). Shown in size 36/38.

Information in the patterns is listed in the same sequence, as follows: measurements for the first indicated size appear before the parenthesis; measurements for the other sizes are given in parentheses and separated by a comma. If there is only one number given in the instructions, it applies to all sizes.

The sizes of all garments are based on average women's sizes, as shown in the table above. The table shows exact body measurements and does not include extra length for seams or comfort when wearing. By contrast, information in the patterns does take these increases into account. Due to differences in design, these increases may differ from one garment to another.

Word of Advice: To make sure the finished garment fits properly, compare the pattern measurements with the measurements of a garment in your own closet that you are comfortable wearing. Use this comparison to help you select the size of the garment you decide to knit.

GAUGE

It is important to knit a gauge swatch before beginning any project; otherwise, the garment simply won't fit properly. Try using different needle sizes to knit the gauge swatch until the sample matches the required number of stitches and rows in the project. If you want fewer stitches per inch/cm, use larger needles or knit loosely; if you want more stitches per inch/cm, use smaller needles or knit tightly. Keep your gauge swatch for blocking.

CHARTS

Charts are helpful for following color work and other stitch patterns at a glance. When knitting back and forth in rows, read the chart from right to left on right side (RS) rows, and from left to right on wrong side (WS) rows. Repeat any stitch and row repeats as directed in the pattern. To keep track of your place, stick a self-adhesive note on the chart under the row you are working on and move the note after every row.

EDGE STITCHES

Adding an edge stitch to your work neatens the seam and makes it easy to line up the pieces. My favorite technique is knitting the first and last stitch on the right and wrong sides of the work. This decorative "knotted" edge also helps the fabric lie flat.

FAIR ISLE

This technique is used to make patterns with several colors, and involves stranding two or more colors per row. To keep tension even and prevent holes in your knitting, pick up yarns alternately over and under one another, across or around. To keep your work from puckering, stretch the stitches on the needle while you knit so that they are a bit wider than the length of the float at the back of the garment.

SEAMS

Woven This makes an invisible seam between two pieces knitted in stockinette stitch.

With right side (RS) of both pieces facing, line up edges so that they are even and insert needle under horizontal bar in one piece, between the first and second stitches. Bring needle up and over, inserting it into corresponding bar on other piece. Pull yarn gently until sides meet. Continue in this manner, alternating from side to side.

Crocheted This makes a seam between two pieces knit in any pattern.

With wrong side (WS) of both pieces facing, line up edges so that they are even, and insert hook into 2nd stitch in one piece and corresponding stitch on other piece. Pull yarn through and slip stitch through both pieces along edge until sides meet. Fasten off.

BLOCKING

This is an important step in finishing the knitting process and the best way to shape pattern pieces and make knitted edges smooth before sewing pieces together. Choose your method of blocking according to the label on your yarn. If you are in doubt, do a test block on your gauge swatch.

CLEANING

• Check the label on your yarn to determine the best way of washing and drying your knitted item. Most of the yarns used in these projects require hand washing or machine washing on a gentle or wool cycle, using mild detergent.

• Do not agitate knitted items, and don't soak them for more than 10 minutes.

• If you are hand washing the items, rinse with lukewarm water to remove detergent.

• Fold wet items in a towel to press out water, and then lay flat to dry in an area that is away from direct heat and light.

YARNS

• The yarns listed in these projects are suggestions; feel free to substitute, according to your preference and availability.

• Remember that you'll need to knit to the given gauge in order to obtain the given measurements with a different yarn, so adjust gauge accordingly.

• Consider whether you'll need to adjust the quantity of yarn for your project in advance, especially if you are ordering your yarn online.

Lovely Additions

CROCHETED FLOWER
(Crocheting stamens/petals in a round)

With RS of flower center facing, insert hook, from top to bottom (pointing to the center) in next unused loop of round 1/round 2 of flower center, slip stitch.

Chain as instructed in first row of stamen/petal.

Turn flower center (WS facing) and work second row of stamen/petal as indicated.

Slip stitch in same stitch as at beginning of first row of stamen/petal.

POMPOM

Copy the disk template (page 82) onto tracing paper. Cut out and transfer twice to cardboard; then cut out two cardboard disks.

Lay cardboard disks on top of each other and line up center holes. Thread a needle with a double strand of yarn about 16"/4.9m long, and wrap disks by drawing yarn up through holes in center of disks and around disks' outer edge. Continue wrapping yarn snugly, keeping strands close together until hole is filled.

Insert scissors between disks and cut yarn all around.

Cut a 39"/99cm piece of yarn, slip it between the disks and tie it tightly around middle of pompom, between the two disks. Cut yarn, leaving 20"/50cm tails for attaching the pompom. Remove cardboard disks and trim yarn to make pompom even.

Fluff up with a little steam.

11

Advanced Knitting Stitches and Techniques

CABLE TWIST-CROSSING TO THE LEFT USING 18 STITCHES

Slip next 9 stitches onto cable needle and hold at front of work.

Knit next 9 stitches, pulling yarn tightly to close gap.

Slip 9 stitches from cable needle back to left needle.

Knit these stitches.

CABLE TWIST-CROSSING TO THE RIGHT USING 18 STITCHES

Slip next 9 stitches onto cable needle and hold at back of work.

Knit next 9 stitches, pulling yarn tightly to close gap.

DOUBLE INCREASE

Knit through the back loop.

Slip 9 stitches from cable needle back to left needle.

While keeping loop on left needle, yarn over working yarn on right needle.

Insert right needle knitwise into same stitch.

Knit these stitches.

Knit.

Three stitches stand on the stitch. This increases 2 stitches at a time.

DOUBLE LEFT-SLANTING DECREASE

Insert right needle knitwise, and slip stitch onto right needle.

Insert right needle knitwise into next 2 stitches.

Knit 2 stitches together.

Pass slipped stitch from right needle over two knitted-together stitches.

One stitch stands on 3 stitches with left slope.

DOUBLE RIGHT-SLANTING DECREASE

Insert right needle knitwise into 3 stitches.

Knit 3 stitches together.

One stitch stands on 3 stitches with right slope.

DRAWSTRING CASING

Pick up and knit, inserting needle through stitches in second row back from knitting as follows:

Insert right needle from front to back into next stitch in second row back from knitting, pull it to front of work, and yarn over.

Pull yarn through this stitch.

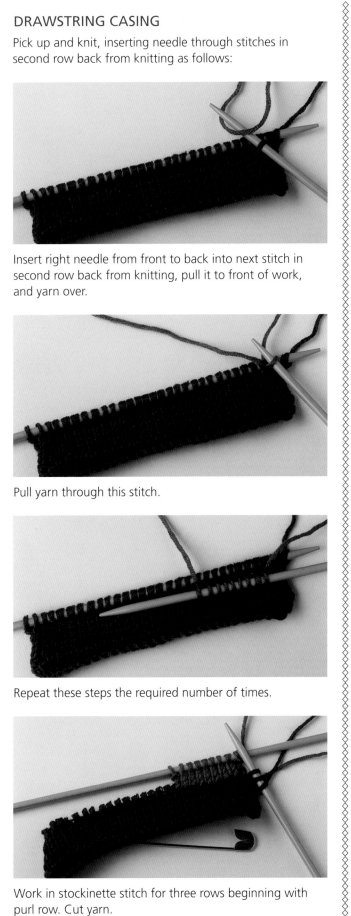

Repeat these steps the required number of times.

Work in stockinette stitch for three rows beginning with purl row. Cut yarn.

Knit together each last row stitch of drawstring casing with corresponding last row stitch of work, as follows:

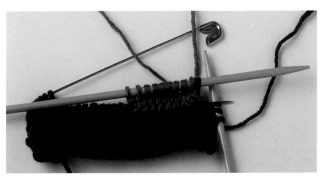

Transfer next stitch from stitch holder to left needle.

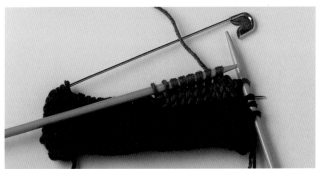

Insert right needle knitwise and knit this stitch and its corresponding casing stitch together.

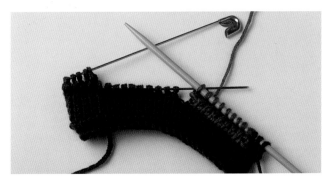

Repeat these steps to end of casing.

ELONGATED STITCH FOR CIRCULAR KNITTING

HORIZONTAL TUCK PATTERN FOR CIRCULAR KNITTING

Insert right needle from back of work to front, into next stitch two rounds below.

Yarn over twice.

Insert right needle from front of work to back, into same stitch at previous round and pull this stitch back (3 rounds below stitch).

Place pulled stitch to left needle.

Knit next stitch.
Repeat these steps to end of round.
On next round, drop 2 yarn overs and knit next stitch.
Repeat previous step to end of round.

Insert right needle purlwise and knit pulled stitch and next stitch together.

SHORT ROWS

Wrap and turn on knit side

Knit through the back loop.

Bring yarn forward.

Slip stitch back to left needle and bring yarn back.

Turn work and purl next stitch.

Wrap and turn on purl side

Bring yarn forward and slip next stitch purlwise to right needle.

Bring yarn back.

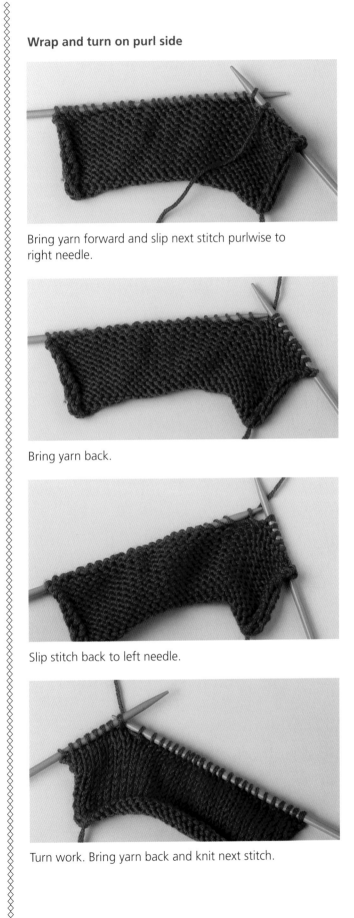

Slip stitch back to left needle.

Turn work. Bring yarn back and knit next stitch.

PICKING UP WRAPPED STITCH ON KNIT SIDE

Pick up wrap with right needle from front to back.

Insert right needle into wrapped stitch.

Knit wrap and stitch together.

PICKING UP WRAPPED STITCH ON PURL SIDE

Pick up wrap with right needle from back to front.

Transfer wrap onto left needle.

Purl together wrap and wrapped stitch.

RIDGED OR VERTICAL DOUBLE DECREASE

Insert right needle knitwise into 2 stitches.

Slip two stitches simultaneously onto right needle.

Insert right needle knitwise into next stitch.

Knit.

Insert left needle simultaneously into slipped stitches. Pass both stitches over knit stitch.

One stitch stands on 3 stitches. The middle stitch is on near side.

PICK UP AND KNIT

Insert needle into stitch indicated and grab yarn.

Pull yarn through.

Insert needle into next stitch.

Knit.

Repeat last 2 steps the required number of times.

WRAP STITCH (RELIEF PATTERN)

Insert right needle between next third and fourth stitches.

Grab working yarn.

Pull a long stitch and leave it on right needle.

Knit each of next 3 stitches that have been wrapped by the long stitch.

Special Crochet Techniques

2-STITCH WIDE LEFT FOLD
Each fold consists of six stitches and one row.

With right side of work facing, insert hook from front to back into next stitch at row indicated.

Skip next two stitches and insert hook from back to front into next stitch (third stitch from hook).

Insert hook from front to back into next stitch.

Grab yarn and draw through work.

Draw yarn through all stitches and through loop on hook.

Insert hook from front to back into back loop of next stitch.

Insert hook from front to back into next unused stitch (fourth stitch from hook).

Grab yarn and draw through work.

Draw yarn through all stitches and through loop on hook. Repeat all steps to make required number of folds.

2-STITCH WIDE RIGHT FOLD

Each fold consists of six stitches and one row.

With right side of work facing, insert hook from front to back into front loop of fifth stitch from hook at row indicated.

Insert hook from front to back into first stitch of fold (stitch corresponding to fifth stitch of fold).

Grab yarn and draw through work.

Draw yarn through all stitches and through loop on hook.

Insert hook from front to back into next stitch, from back to front into third stitch of fold, and from front to back into second stitch of fold (stitches corresponding to sixth stitch of fold).

Grab yarn and draw through work.

Draw yarn through all stitches and through loop on hook. Repeat steps to make required number of folds.

FAUX PLISSE FOLD

With right side of work facing and bottom to your left, insert hook under left leg of indicated stitch and under right leg of same row/round next stitch and grab yarn.

Draw yarn through loops.

Insert hook under left leg of stitch below and under right leg of corresponding stitch and grab yarn.

Draw yarn through these loops and through loop on hook.

Repeat last 2 steps the required number of times.

OVERLAY CHAIN STITCH

Insert hook into work, from front to back, into stitch indicated and grab working yarn.

Draw yarn through work.

Insert hook into next stitch, yarn over.

Draw yarn through work

and through loop on hook.

Repeat last 3 steps the required number of times.

Terms and Abbreviations

approx	approximately
beg	begin
C18B	Cable Twist–crossing to the right using 18 stitches
C18F	Cable Twist–crossing to the left using 18 stitches
ch(s)	chain stitch(es)
cm	centimeter(s)
dec	decrease
g	grams
k	knit
k2tog	knit 2 together
lp(s)	loop(s)
m	meter(s)
mm	millimeter
overlay ch(s)	overlay chain stitch(es)
oz	ounce
p	purl
p2tog	purl 2 together
prev	previous
rem	remaining
rep	repeat
rnd(s)	round(s)
RS	right side
sc	single crochet
sk	skip
skp	slip one, knit one, pass slipped st over knit stitch
sl st	slip stitch
st(s)	stitch(es)
St st	stockinette stitch
tog	together
WS	wrong side
yd	yard
yo	yarn over
***(**)**	repeat instructions following the single (double) asterisk as many times as written

Ultimate Urban Overcoat

This gorgeous coat is perfect for urban work or play. It features a dramatic collar, gorgeous cuffs and clean styling. Complement the bold buttons with a thick black belt for cinching, and you're ready to play in the concrete jungle!

EXPERIENCE LEVEL

■■■□ Intermediate

SIZES

> 36/38 (40/42, 44/46). Shown in size 44/46.

FINISHED FLAT MEASUREMENTS

> Chest at underarms: 19"/48cm (20½"/52cm, 22"/56cm)

> Length: 37"/94cm (39"/99cm, 39"/99cm)

> Upper arms: 7½"/19cm (8¼"/21cm, 9"/23cm)

MATERIALS AND TOOLS

> Yarn A: **SUPER BULKY 6** 1339yd/1222m of bulky yarn, Peruvian highland wool, in dark gray

> Yarn B: **SUPER BULKY 6** 21yd/19m of super bulky yarn, wool/nylon, in black

> Size 10 (6mm) straight knitting needles OR SIZE TO OBTAIN GAUGE

> Size 10 (6mm) by 24" to 32" circular knitting needles OR SIZE TO OBTAIN GAUGE

> Stitch holder

> Six buttons, 1¼"/3cm diameter

> Scissors

> Yarn needle

> Sewing needle

GAUGE

> With Yarn A in Relief Pattern, 18 sts and 20 rows to 4"/10cm

> With Yarn A in St st, 15 sts and 20 rows to 4"/10cm

> With Yarn A in (k3, p3) rib pattern, 18 sts and 20 rows to 4"/10cm

Measurements

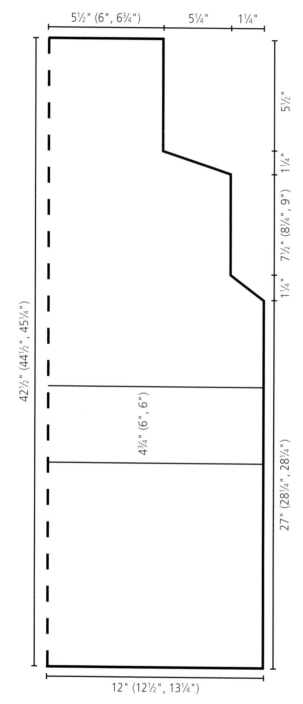

5½" (6", 6¾")   5¼"   1¼"

5½"

1¼"

7½" (8¼", 9")

1¼"

42½" (44½", 45¼")

4¾" (6", 6")

27" (28¼", 28¼")

12" (12½", 13¼")

RELIEF PATTERN

Pattern consists of 3 sts and 8 rows.

Row 1: K all sts.

Row 2: K1, p to last st, k1.

Row 3: *Insert right needle between next 3rd and 4th sts, pull a long st and leave it on right needle, k each of next 3 sts that were wrapped by the long st, rep from * number of times indicated.

Row 4: K1, p to last st, purling tog pulled long st with its next st, k1.

Instructions

BACK

With straight needles and Yarn A, cast on 91 (97, 103) sts.

Rows 1–2: K all sts.

Row 3 (WS): K1, p to last st, k1.

Beg Relief Pattern

Pattern consists of 3 sts and 8 rows.

Work in Relief Pattern for next 68 rows as follows:

Rows 1–2: Work rows 1–2 of Relief Pattern.

Row 3: K4, work row 3 of Relief Pattern, rep from * 28 (30, 32) times, k3.

Row 4: Work row 4 of Relief Pattern.

Rows 5–6: Rep rows 1–2.

Row 7: K5, work row 3 of Relief Pattern, rep from * 27 (29, 31) times, k5.

Row 8: Rep row 4.

Rep rows 1–8 seven more times.

Rep rows 1–4 one more time. Work in St st for next 4 rows.

Work in rib pattern for next 24 (30, 30) rows as follows: k8, (p3, k3) rib 12 (13, 14) times, p3, k8.

Work in St st for next 4 rows.

Beg Relief Pattern

Rep rows 1–8 two more times.

Armhole shaping

Work next 6 rows as follows:

Row 1: K1, k2tog, k to last 3 sts, skp, k1.

Row 2: K1, p2tog, p to last 3 sts, p2tog, k1—87 (93, 99) sts.

Row 3: K1, k2tog, k2, work row 3 of Relief Pattern, rep from * 26 (28, 30) times, k1, skp, k1.

Row 4: K1, p2tog, work row 4 of Relief Pattern to last 4 sts, p1, p2tog, k1.

Rows 5–6: Rep rows 1–2—79 (85, 91) sts.

Armhole ribbing

Work next rows as follows:

Row 1: K1, (k3, p3) rib twice, k2, work row 3 of Relief Pattern, rep from * 16 (18, 20) times, k3, (p3, k3) rib twice, k1.

Row 2: K1, (p3, k3) rib twice, work row 4 of Relief Pattern to last 14 sts, p1, (k3, p3) rib twice, k1.

Row 3: K1, (k3, p3) rib twice, k to last 13 sts, (p3, k3) rib twice, k1.

Row 4: K1, (p3, k3) rib twice, p to last 13 sts, (k3, p3) rib twice, k1.

Row 5: K1, (k3, p3) rib twice, k3, work row 3 of Relief Pattern, rep from * 16 (18, 20) times, k2, (p3, k3) rib twice, k1.

Rows 6–8: Rep rows 2–4.

Rep rows 1–8 two more times.

For size 40/42 only
Rep rows 1–4 one more time.

For size 44/46 only
Rep rows 1–8 one more time.

Shoulder shaping

Work next 6 short rows as follows:

Short rows
Row 1: K21, join Yarn B and k37 (k43, k49), join Yarn A (other ball) and k14, wrap and turn.

Row 2: Work back the other way; with Yarn A, p14; with Yarn B, p37 (p43, p49); with Yarn A, p14, wrap and turn.

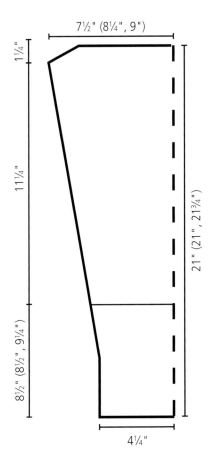

7½" (8¼", 9")

1¼"

11¼"

21" (21, 21¾")

8½" (8½", 9¼")

4¼"

Row 3: Work back the other way; with Yarn A, k14; with Yarn B, k37 (k43, k49); with Yarn A, k7, wrap and turn.

Row 4: Work back the other way; with Yarn A, p7; with Yarn B, p37 (p43, p49); with Yarn A, p7; wrap and turn.

Row 5: Work back the other way; with Yarn A, k7; with Yarn B, k37 (k43, k49); with Yarn A, k to end, knitting each wrap and st tog.

Row 6: With Yarn A, BO 21 sts for right shoulder in purl; with Yarn B, p36 (p42, p48); with Yarn A, p to end, purling each wrap and st tog.

With Yarn A, BO 21 sts for left shoulder. Transfer rem 37 (43, 49) sts to stitch holder.

FRONT
Left front
With Yarn A and straight needles, cast on 55 (58, 61) sts.

Rows 1–2: K all sts.

Row 3 (WS): K9 for border, p to last st, k1.

Beg Relief Pattern
Pattern consists of 3 sts and 8 rows.

Work in Relief Pattern for next 68 rows as follows:

Row 1: K all sts.

Row 2: K9 for border, p to last st, k1.

Row 3: K4, work row 3 of Relief Pattern, rep from * 13 (14, 15) times, k12 (k3, k9 for border).

Row 4: K9 for border, work row 4 of Relief Pattern.

Rows 5–6: Rep rows 1–2.

Row 7: K5, work row 3 of Relief Pattern, rep from * 13 (14, 15) times, k11.

Row 8: Rep row 4.

Rep rows 1–8 seven more times.

Rep rows 1–4 one more time.

Work in St st for next 4 rows.

Work in rib pattern for next 24 (30, 30) rows as follows:

Row 1: K2 (k5, k8), (p3, k3) rib 6 times, p3, k14.

Row 2: K9 for border, p5, k3, (p3, k3) rib 6 times, p2 (p5, p8).

Rep rows 1–2 eleven (fourteen, fourteen) times.

Work in St st for next 4 rows.

Beg Relief Pattern
Rep rows 1–8 three times.

Armhole shaping
Work next 6 rows as follows:

Row 1: K1, k2tog, k to end.

Row 2: K9 for border, p to last 3 sts, p2tog, k1—53 (56, 59) sts.

Row 3: K1, k2tog, k2, work row 3 of Relief Pattern, rep from * 12 (13, 14) times, k12.

Row 4: K9 for border, p3, work row 4 of Relief Pattern to last 3 sts, p2tog, k1.

Rows 5–6: Rep rows 1–2—49 (52, 55) sts.

Armhole ribbing
Work next rows as follows:

Row 1: K1, (k3, p3) rib twice, k3, work row 3 of Relief Pattern, rep from * 7 (8, 9) times, k12.

Row 2: K9 for border, work row 4 of Relief Pattern to last 15 sts, p2, (k3, p3) rib twice, k1.

Row 3: K1, (k3, p3) rib twice, k to end.

Row 4: K9 for border, p to last 13 sts, (k3, p3) rib twice, k1.

Rep rows 1–4 five more times.

For size 40/42 only
Rep rows 1–4 one more time.

For size 44/46 only
Rep rows 1–4 two more times.

Shoulder shaping
Work next 6 short rows as follows:

Short rows
Row 1: K21, join Yarn B and k19 (k22, k25), join Yarn A (other ball) and k9.

Row 2: With Yarn A, k9 for border; with Yarn B, p19 (p22, p25); with Yarn A, p14, wrap and turn.

Row 3: Work back the other way, with Yarn A, k14, with Yarn B, k19 (k22, k25), with Yarn A, k9.

Row 4: With Yarn A, k9, with Yarn B, p19 (p22, p25), with Yarn A, p7, wrap and turn.

Row 5: Work back the other way; with Yarn A, k7; with Yarn B, k19 (k22, k25); with Yarn A, k9.

Row 6: With Yarn A, BO 9 sts of border; with Yarn B, p18 (p21, p24); with Yarn A, p to end, purling each wrap and st tog.

With Yarn A, BO 21 sts for left shoulder. Transfer rem 19 (22, 25) sts onto stitch holder.

Right front
Work to correspond to left front, reversing shaping.

Work skp instead of k2tog for armhole shaping.

Work short rows of right shoulder shaping on RS.

Note Instructions are given for the border only. Work the rest of the row as indicated for left front.

Work 5 buttonholes at right front border. Beg at 26th (28th, 32nd) row and each next 30th (32nd, 34th) row, as follows:

Buttonhole Row 1: K 3 sts, BO 3 sts for buttonhole, k3.

Buttonhole Row 2: K3, CO 3 sts for buttonhole, k3.

SLEEVES
With Yarn A and straight needles, cast on 39 sts.

Work in (k3, p3) rib pattern for next 14 (14, 18) rows.

Cont to work in (k3, p3) rib pattern for next 28 rows, inc 1 st at each side (Inc Row) of 13th and 27th rows (twice in total), as follows:

Inc Row: K1, inc 1, (k3, p3) rib to last 2 sts, inc 1, k1—43 sts.

For size 36/38 only
Work in St st for next 2 rows.

For size 40/42 only
Row 1: K1, (inc 1, k7) 5 times, inc 1, k1—49 sts.

Row 2: P all sts.

For size 44/46 only
Row 1: K1, inc 1, k1, (inc 1, k3) 9 times, (inc 1, k1) twice—55 sts.

Row 2: P all sts.

Beg Relief Pattern
Beg with 1st row of Relief Pattern, work in Relief Pattern on middle 39 (45, 51) sts for next 12 rows, inc 1 st at each side (Inc Row) of 1st and 7th rows (twice in total) as follows:

Row 1 (Inc Row): K1, inc 1, k to last 2 sts, inc 1, k1—45 (51, 57) sts.

Row 7 (Inc Row): K1, inc 1, k1, work row 3 of Relief Pattern, rep from * 13 (15, 17) times, k1, inc 1, k1—47 (53, 59) sts.

Beg with 1st row of Relief Pattern, work in Relief Pattern on middle 45 (51, 57) sts for next 20 rows, inc 1 st at each side (Inc Row) of 1st, 7th, 13th and 19th rows (4 times in total) as follows:

Row 1 (Inc Row): K1, inc 1, k to last 2 sts, inc 1, k1—49 (55, 61) sts.

Row 7 (Inc Row): K1, inc 1, work row 3 of Relief Pattern, rep from * 15 (17, 19) times, inc 1, k1—51 (57, 63) sts.

Row 13 (Inc Row): K1, inc 1, k to last 2 sts, inc 1, k1—53 (59, 65) sts.

Row 19 (Inc Row): K1, inc 1, k2, work row 3 of Relief Pattern, rep from * 15 (17, 19) times, k2, inc 1, k1—55 (61, 67) sts.

Beg with 1st row of Relief Pattern, work in Relief Pattern on middle 51 (57, 63) sts for next 16 rows, inc 1 st at each side (Inc Row) of 5th and 11th rows (twice in total) as follows:

Row 5 (Inc Row): K1, inc 1, k to last 2 sts, inc 1, k1—57 (63, 69) sts.

Row 11 (Inc Row): K1, inc 1, k1, work row 3 of Relief Pattern, rep from * 17 (19, 21) times, k1, inc 1, k1—59 (65, 71) sts.

Work in St st for 2 more rows, inc 1 st at each side of 1st row—61 (67, 73) sts.

Sleeve top shaping
Dec 1 st at each side each 2nd row for 6 times as follows:

Row 1: K1, k2tog, k2 work row 3 of Relief Pattern, rep from * 17 (19, 21) times, k2, skp, k1—59 (65, 71) sts.

Row 2: K1, p2tog, work row 4 of Relief Pattern to last 4 sts, p1, p2tog, k1—57 (63, 69) sts.

Row 3: K1, k2tog, k to last 3 sts, skp, k1—55 (61, 67) sts.

Row 4: K1, p2tog, p to last 3 sts, p2tog, k1—53 (59, 65) sts.

Rep rows 3–4 once more—49 (55, 61) sts.

BO all sts.

FAUX KARAKUL COLLAR
Transfer all rem sts of left front, back, and right front from stitch holders onto circular needles—75 (87, 99) sts.

Join Yarn B and work in St st for next 20 rows.

Work next 2 rows as follows:

Buttonhole Row 1: K3 sts, BO 3 sts for buttonhole, k to end.

Buttonhole Row 2: P to last 6 sts, CO 3 sts for buttonhole, p3.

Work in St st for 3 more rows.

BO all sts in purl.

FINISHING
Sew shoulder seams.

Set sleeves by sewing bound-off sts at top of sleeve to bound-off armhole sts.

Sew side seams.

Sew buttons on left front border corresponding to buttonholes.

This project was knit with

(A) 11 (12, 13) balls of Berroco Peruvia Quick Gris Marengo, 100% Peruvian highland wool, bulky weight, approx 3.5oz/100g = 103yd/94m per ball, color 9117

(B) 4 balls of Lion Sasha Yarn, 96% wool/4% nylon, super bulky weight, approx 1.75oz/50 grams = 21yd/19m, color #690-153

Stylish City Sweater

This bold design is made with organic, earthy red wool. The pattern is knitted vertically, beginning from the sleeves, while the front and back are knitted as a single piece. Easy to knit thanks to minimal shaping, it is perfectly accented with a thick wraparound belt.

EXPERIENCE LEVEL

◼◼◼◻ Intermediate

SIZES

> 36 (38/40, 42/44). Shown in size 36.

FINISHED FLAT MEASUREMENTS

> Chest at underarms: 17"/43cm (18½"/47cm, 20"/50cm)
> Length: 25½"/65cm (26½"/67cm, 27½"/70cm)
> Upper arms: 10¼"/26cm

MATERIALS AND TOOLS

> Yarn A: **SUPER BULKY 6** 1,110yd/1,020m of medium weight yarn, organic wool, in dark red

> Yarn B: **SUPER BULKY 6** 230yds/210m of super-fine/fingering weight yarn super kid mohair/silk, in dark red

> Size 10 (6mm) straight knitting needles OR SIZE TO OBTAIN GAUGE

> Size E/4 (3.5) crochet hook OR SIZE TO OBTAIN GAUGE

> Scissors

> Yarn needle

GAUGE

> With Yarn A in Garter st, 14 sts and 26 rows to 4"/10cm

Measurements

◇◇◇◇◇◇◇◇◇◇◇◇◇◇◇◇

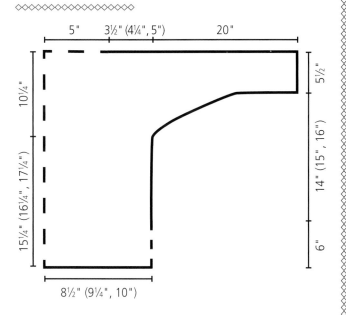

5" 3½" (4¼", 5") 20"

10¼"

5½"

14" (15", 16")

15¼" (16¼", 17¼")

6"

8½" (9¼", 10")

Instructions

◇◇◇◇◇◇◇◇◇◇◇◇◇◇◇◇

Note This sweater was knit vertically, beginning from the sleeves. The front and back are identical.

FRONT/BACK

Left/right sleeve (from bottom to top)
With Yarn A, cast on 20 sts.

Beg at bottom of left/right sleeve, work in Garter st (k all sts) for next 28 rows.

*Inc Row: K to last 2 sts, inc 1, k1.

Work in Garter st (k all sts) for next 17 rows.

Rep from * 2 more times—23 sts.

Rep Inc Row one more time—24 sts.

Work in Garter st (k all sts) 3 more rows.

**Next Row: Rep Inc Row.

Work in Garter st (k all sts) for next 3 rows.

Rep from ** 10 more times—35 sts.

Rep Inc Row once more. Cont and cast on more 54 sts for front/back—90 sts.

Front/back
Beg at WS row, cont and work in Garter st (k all sts) for next 32 (38, 44) rows. Cut Yarn A.

Join Yarn B, beg at WS row (p all sts), and work in St st for next 2 rows. Cut Yarn B.

*Next Row: Join Yarn A, P all sts.

Work in Garter st (k all sts) for next 5 rows. Cut Yarn A.

Join Yarn B, beg at WS row (p all sts), work in St st for next 2 rows. Cut Yarn B.

Rep from * 5 more times.

Rep Next Row one more time.

Work in Garter st (k all sts) for next 31 (37, 43) rows.

Right/left sleeve (from top to bottom)
BO 54 (58, 62) sts of front/back, cont and k2tog, k to end—35 sts.

*Work in Garter st (k all sts) for next 3 rows.

Dec Row: K1, k2tog, k to end.

Rep from * 10 more times—24 sts.

Work in Garter st (k all sts) 3 more rows.

**Next Row: Rep Dec Row.

Work in Garter st (k all sts) for next 17 rows.

Rep from ** 2 more times—21 sts.

Rep Dec Row one more time—20 sts.

Work in Garter st (k all sts) for next 27 (31, 35) rows.

BO all sts.

FINISHING

Middle front/back gather
With RS of sweater front/back facing, bottom close to you, using Yarn A and crochet hook, work overlay ch sts as follows: beg 3 rows to the right from 1st B-yarn stripe at front/back of sweater, work 23 overlay ch sts along front/back middle part, inserting hook in each 2nd row 25th st from top of sweater, finishing 2 rows left from last B-yarn stripe at front/back of sweater. Fasten off.

With RS of sweater front/back facing, bottom close to you, using Yarn A and crochet hook, work overlay ch sts as follows: beg 3 rows to the right from 1st B-yarn stripe at front/back of sweater, work 23 overlay ch sts along front/back middle part, inserting hook in each 2nd row 25th st from top of sweater, finishing 2 rows left from last B-yarn stripe at front/back of sweater. Fasten off.

Left/right sleeve and shoulder stripe
With RS of sweater front facing, bottom close to you and Yarn B, beg at left sleeve bottom/5 rows left of last B-yarn stripe at front of sweater, pick up and k160 (172, 184) sts, inserting needle through every other st along left sleeve/right shoulder and left shoulder/right sleeve, finishing 5 rows right from 1st B-yarn stripe at front of sweater/ right sleeve bottom.

Beg at WS row, work in St st for next 2 rows.

BO loosely all sts.

Beg at WS row, work in St st for next 2 rows.

BO loosely all sts.

Left sleeve and shoulder seam/right sleeve and shoulder seam
With RS of sweater back facing, bottom close to you, using Yarn B and crochet hook, beg 5 rows left from last B-yarn stripe at back of sweater/right sleeve bottom, work 160 (166, 172) overlay ch sts along left shoulder/right sleeve and left sleeve/ right shoulder, inserting hook through every other st of each row and its corresponding bound-off st at left sleeve and shoulder stripe/right sleeve and shoulder stripe. Fasten off.

Side and sleeve seams
With WS of front/back facing, bottom to your right, beg at 22nd st (6"/15cm up) from tunic bottom, sew side and sleeve seams.

This project was knit with

(A) 6 (7, 8) balls of LB Collection Organic Wool Yarn, 100% organic wool, medium worsted weight, approx 3.5oz/100g = 185yd/170m, color 481-114

(B) 1 ball of Cascade Yarns Kid Seta Solid Yarn, 70% super kid mohair/30% silk, super-fine/fingering weight, approx .88oz/25g = 230yds/210m, color 681

Autumn Butterfly Vest

This striking vest features earthy colors knit in flattering vertical lines. The fitted waist contrasts beautifully with the loose sleeves, creating a look that is ethnic and interesting, trendy and sophisticated.

EXPERIENCE LEVEL

◼◼◼☐ Intermediate

SIZES

> 36 (38/40, 42/44). Shown in size 36.

FINISHED FLAT MEASUREMENTS

> Chest at underarms: 16"/40cm (17½"/44.5cm, 19"/48cm)

> Length: 21¼"/54cm (21½"/55cm, 22½"/57cm)

> Upper arms: 9¼"/23.5cm

MATERIALS AND TOOLS

> Yarn A: **SUPER BULKY 6** 980yd/900m of wool yarn, medium weight, in variegated purple, yellow, green and beige

> Yarn B: **SUPER BULKY 6** 215yd/198m of super fine alpaca/Peruvian wool yarn, medium weight, in dusty green

> Yarn C: **MEDIUM 4** 215yd/198m of super fine alpaca/Peruvian wool yarn, medium weight, in dark green

> Yarn D: **MEDIUM 4** 215yd/198m of super fine alpaca/Peruvian wool yarn, medium weight, in deep green

> Size 9 (5.5mm) straight knitting needles OR SIZE TO OBTAIN GAUGE

> Size 8 (5mm) by 24" to 32" circular knitting needles OR SIZE TO OBTAIN GAUGE

> Size E/4 (3.5) crochet hook OR SIZE TO OBTAIN GAUGE

> 2 stitch markers

> Three buttons, ¼"/0.5cm diameter

> Scissors

> Yarn needle

> Sewing needle and thread

GAUGE

> With Yarn A, in St st, 18 sts and 20 rows to 4"/10cm

Measurements

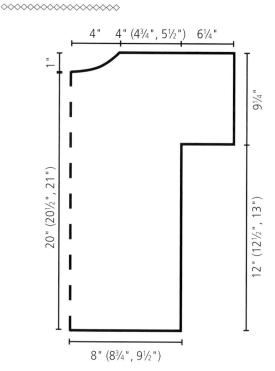

4" 4" (4¾", 5½") 6¼"

1"

20" (20½", 21")

9¼"

12" (12½", 13")

8" (8¾", 9½")

Instructions

Note This vest is knit vertically beginning from the sleeves.

BACK
Right back sleeve (from bottom to top)

With Yarn A and straight needles, cast on 42 sts.

*Work in St st for next 4 rows. Cut Yarn A.

Join Yarn B. Work in Garter st (k all sts) for next 2 rows. Cut Yarn B.

Rep from * 5 more times.

Join Yarn A. Work in St st for 3 more rows. End at RS row. Cont and cast on 54 (56, 58) more sts for back—96 (98, 100) sts.

Body back
Beg at WS row, cont and work in St st for next 3 rows. Cut Yarn A.

Join Yarn C. Work in Garter st (k all sts) for next 2 rows. Cut Yarn C.

Join Yarn A. Work in St st for next 6 (8, 10) rows. Cut Yarn A.

Join Yarn C. Work in Garter st (k all sts) for next 2 rows. Cut Yarn C.

Join Yarn A. Work in St st for next 6 (8, 10) rows. Cut Yarn A.

Join Yarn D. Work in Garter st (k all sts) for next 2 rows. Cut Yarn D.

Join Yarn A. Work in St st for next 4 rows.

Back neck shaping
Row 1: With Yarn A, k1, k2tog, k to end.

Row 2: P all sts. Cut Yarn A.

Row 3: Join Yarn C. K1, k2tog, k to end.

Row 4: P all sts. Cut Yarn C.

Rep rows 1–2 three more times (cut Yarn A only after done with repeats)—91 (93, 95) sts.

Rows 11–12: Join Yarn D. Work in Garter st (k all sts) for next 2 rows. Cut Yarn D.

Rows 13–18: Join Yarn A. Work in St st for next 6 rows. Cut Yarn.

Rep rows 11–18 two more times.

Rows 35–36: Join Yarn D. Work in Garter st (k all sts) for 2 more rows. Cut Yarn D.

Row 37: Join Yarn A. K1, inc 1, k to end.

Row 38: P all sts.

Rep rows 37–38 two more times. Cut Yarn A.

Row 43: Join Yarn C. K1, inc 1, k to end.

Row 44: P all sts. Cut Yarn C.

Rep rows 37–38 one more time (don't cut Yarn A)—96 (98, 100) sts.

Work in St st for next 4 rows. Cut Yarn A.

Join Yarn D. Work in Garter st (k all sts) for next 2 rows. Cut Yarn D.

Join Yarn A. Work in St st for next 6 (8, 10) rows. Cut Yarn A.

Join Yarn C. Work in Garter st (k all sts) for next 2 rows. Cut Yarn C.

Join Yarn A. Work in St st for next 6 (8, 10) rows. Cut Yarn A.

Join Yarn C. Work in Garter st (k all sts) for next 2 rows. Cut Yarn C.

Join Yarn A. Work in St st for next 3 rows.

Left back sleeve (from top to bottom)
BO 54 (56, 58) sts of back in purl, cont and p to end— 42 sts.

Work in St st for 2 more rows.

Join Yarn B. Work in Garter st (k all sts) for next 2 rows. Cut Yarn B.

Work in St st for next 4 rows. Cut Yarn A.

Rep from * 5 more times.

BO all sts.

LEFT FRONT
Follow same instruction as for right back until row 11 of back neck shaping.

Cont and work next rows as follows:

Rows 11–12: Join Yarn D. Work in Garter st (k all sts) for next 2 rows. Cut Yarn D.

Rows 13–18: Join Yarn A. Work in St st for next 6 rows. Cut Yarn A.

Rep rows 11–12 one more time.

Rows 21–23: Join Yarn A. Work in St st for next 3 rows.

BO all sts.

RIGHT FRONT
Follow same instruction as for right back until back neck shaping.

Cont and work next rows as follows:

Row 1: With Yarn A, k to last 3 sts, skp, k1.

Row 2: P all sts. Cut Yarn A.

Row 3: Join Yarn C. K to last 3 sts, skp, k1.

Row 4: P all sts. Cut Yarn C.

Rep rows 1–2 three more times (cut Yarn A only at the end)—91 (93, 95) sts.

Rep rows 11–23 of left front.

BO all sts.

FINISHING
Sew shoulder and sleeve seams.
Sew side and sleeve seams.

Front and neck opening border
2-stitch wide folds
With RS of front facing, bottom to your right, using Yarn C and crochet hook, beg at bottom of the vest and work overlay chs loosely as follows:

Work 4 overlay chs along right front edge inserting hook into each st, then make seven 2-stitch wide left folds, cont and work overlay chs in each st along the same front edge to top then across neck opening edge inserting hook into every other stitch along the neck edge. Cont along left front edge inserting hook into each st from top to point corresponding with topmost fold of right front, make seven 2-stitch wide right folds, cont and work 4 overlay chs to bottom of same edge.

With RS of front facing, bottom to your right, using Yarn A and circular needle, pick up and k along right front edge from bottom to top, then across neck opening edge and along left front edge from top to bottom, inserting needle in back lp of each overlay ch. Mark topmost sts of left/right front.

Row 1: P all sts.

Row 2: K to last st before 1st marked st, inc 1, k marked st, inc 1, k to last st before 2nd marked st, inc 1, k marked st, inc 1, k to end.

Rep rows 1–2 one more time.

Row 5: K all sts.

Row 6: K to last 2 sts before 1st marked st, skp, k marked st, k2tog, k to last 2 sts before 2nd marked st, skp, k marked st, k2tog, k to end.

Row 7: P all sts.

Rep rows 6–7 one more time.

BO all sts.

With WS of front facing, bottom to your right, using Yarn C and crochet hook, fold border in half and work overlay chs along right front edge from bottom to top, then across neck opening edge and along left front edge from top to bottom, inserting hook in BO sts of border and corresponding sts on vest.

Bottom border
With RS of front facing, top close to you, using Yarn C and circular needle, pick up and k all sts across vest bottom, inserting needle in every other st along vest bottom.

Row 1: P all sts.

BO all sts.

Button loops
With WS of front facing, bottom to your left, using Yarn B and crochet hook, insert hook in folded row st of right front border opposite topmost fold, ch10 for 1st button lp, sl st in next st folded row of right front border. *Cont and work 10 overlay chs, inserting hook in each st of

folded row of right front border, ch 10 for next button lp. Rep from * one more time. End with sl st in next st folded row of right front border. Fasten off.

Sew buttons on left front border corresponding to button lps.

This project was knit with

(A) 10 (11, 12) balls of Berroco Jasper Verde Lavras, 100% wool yarn, medium weight, approx 1.75oz/50g = 98yd/90m per ball, color 3833

(B) 1 ball of Berroco Ultra Alpaca Yarn, 50% super fine alpaca/50% Peruvian wool, medium weight, approx 3.5oz/100g = 215yd/198m per ball, color 6249

(C) 1 ball of Berroco Ultra Alpaca Yarn, 50% super fine alpaca/50% Peruvian wool, medium weight, approx 3.5oz/100g = 215yd/198m per ball, color 6218

(D) 1 ball of Berroco Ultra Alpaca Yarn, 50% super fine alpaca/50% Peruvian wool, medium weight, approx 3.5oz/100g = 215yd/198m per ball, color 6210

Seductive Retro Blouse

This fantastically feminine blouse can be transformed to suit as many looks as you like. The body of the blouse is knitted in a lovely polka dot lace pattern. It also includes a long mohair string collar that can be tied in dozens of ways.

EXPERIENCE LEVEL

 Intermediate

SIZES

> 36 (38/40, 42/44). Shown in size 36.

FINISHED FLAT MEASUREMENTS

> Chest at underarms: 17"/43cm (18½"/47cm, 20"/50cm)

> Length (from bottom to neck opening): 24½"/62cm (25"/63.5cm, 25¾"/65.5cm)

> Upper arms: 9"/23cm

MATERIALS AND TOOLS

> Yarn A: **MEDIUM 4** 600yd/552m of medium weight yarn, rayon/linen/silk/nylon, in variegated gray

> Yarn B: **SUPER FINE 1** 230yds/210m of superfine/fingering weight yarn super kid mohair/silk, in light gray

> Size 8 (5mm) straight knitting needles OR SIZE TO OBTAIN GAUGE

> Size 8 (5mm) by 24" to 32" circular knitting needles OR SIZE TO OBTAIN GAUGE

> Size E/4 (3.5mm) crochet hook OR SIZE TO OBTAIN GAUGE

> Yarn needle

> Scissors

GAUGE

> In St st, 18 sts and 20 rows to 4"/10cm

Measurements

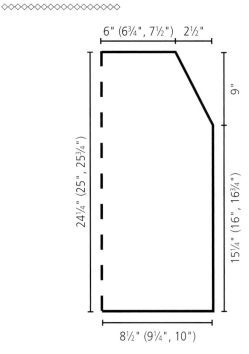

6" (6¾", 7½")   2½"

9"

24¼" (25", 25¾")

15¼" (16", 16¾")

8½" (9¼", 10")

POLKA DOT LACE PATTERN

Pattern consists of 6 sts and 4 rnds

Row 1: P all sts.

Row 2: *Ridged double decrease, k1, double increase in next st, k1, rep from * required number of times.

Row 3: Rep row 1.

Row 4: **Double increase in next st, k1, ridged double decrease, k1, rep from ** required number of times.

Note Row 2 reduces the row stitch count by two and row 4 replaces them.

Instructions

FRONT

With Yarn A and straight needles, cast on 77 (83, 89) sts.

Beg with WS row (p all sts), work in St st for 5 rows.

Beg Polka Dot Lace Pattern

Pattern consists of 6 sts and 4 rows.

Work in Polka Dot Lace Pattern for next 76 (80, 84) rows as follows:

Row 1: K7, rep from Polka Dot Lace Pattern * 10 (11, 12) times, ridged double decrease k7—75 (81, 87) sts.

Row 2: P all sts.

Row 3: K7, rep from Polka Dot Lace Pattern ** 10 (11, 12) times, double increase in next st, k7—77 (83, 89) sts.

Row 4: Rep row 2.

Rep rows 1–4 eighteen (nineteen, twenty) more times.

ARMHOLE SHAPING

Row 1: K1, k2tog, k7, rep from Polka Dot Lace Pattern * 9 (10, 11) times, ridged double decrease, k to last 3 sts, skp, k1—73 (79, 85) sts.

Row 2 and each even row: K1, p to last st, k1.

Row 3: K9, rep from Polka Dot Lace Pattern ** 9 (10, 11) times, double increase in next st, k9—75 (81, 87) sts.

Row 5: K1, k2tog, k6, rep from Polka Dot Lace Pattern * 9 (10, 11) times, ridged double decrease, k to last 3 sts, skp, k1—71 (77, 83) sts.

Row 7: K8, rep from Polka Dot Lace Pattern ** 9 (10, 11) times, double increase in next st, k8—73 (79, 85) sts.

Row 9: K1, k2tog, k5, rep from Polka Dot Lace Pattern * 9 (10, 11) times, ridged double decrease, k to last 3 sts, skp, k1—69 (75, 81) sts.

Row 11: K7, rep from Polka Dot Lace Pattern ** 9 (10, 11) times, double increase in next st, k7—71 (77, 83) sts.

Row 13: K1, k2tog, k7, rep from Polka Dot Lace Pattern * 8 (9, 10) times, ridged double decrease, k to last 3 sts, skp, k1—67 (73, 79) sts.

Row 15: K9, rep from Polka Dot Lace Pattern ** 8 (9, 10) times, double increase in next st, k9—69 (75, 81) sts.

Row 17: K1, k2tog, k6, rep from Polka Dot Lace Pattern * 8 (9, 10) times, ridged double decrease, k to last 3 sts, skp, k1—65 (71, 77) sts.

Row 19: K8, rep from Polka Dot Lace Pattern ** 8 (9, 10) times, double increase in next st, k8—67 (73, 79) sts.

Row 21: K1, k2tog, k5, rep from Polka Dot Lace Pattern * 8 (9, 10) times, ridged double decrease, k to last 3 sts, skp, k1—63 (69, 75) sts.

Row 23: K7, rep from Polka Dot Lace Pattern ** 8 (9, 10) times, double increase in next st, k7—65 (71, 77) sts.

Row 25: K1, k2tog, k7, rep from Polka Dot Lace Pattern * 7 (8, 9) times, ridged double decrease, k to last 3 sts, skp, k1—61 (67, 73) sts.

Row 27: K9, rep from Polka Dot Lace Pattern ** 7 (8, 9) times, double increase in next st, k9—63 (69, 75) sts.

Row 29: K1, k2tog, k6, rep from Polka Dot Lace Pattern * 7 (8, 9) times, ridged double decrease, k to last 3 sts, skp, k1—59 (65, 71) sts.

Row 31: K8, rep from Polka Dot Lace Pattern ** 7 (8, 9) times, double increase in next st, k8—61 (67, 73) sts.

Row 33: K1, k2tog, k5, rep from Polka Dot Lace Pattern * 7 (8, 9) times, ridged double decrease, k to last 3 sts, skp, k1—57 (63, 69) sts.

Row 35: K7, rep from Polka Dot Lace Pattern ** 7 (8, 9) times, double increase in next st, k7—59 (65, 71) sts.

Row 37: K1, k2tog, k7, rep from Polka Dot Lace Pattern * 6 (7, 8) times, ridged double decrease, k to last 3 sts, skp, k1—55 (61, 67) sts.

Row 39: K9, rep from Polka Dot Lace Pattern ** 6 (7, 8) times, double increase in next st, k9—57 (63, 69) sts.

Row 41: K1, k2tog, k6, rep from Polka Dot Lace Pattern *

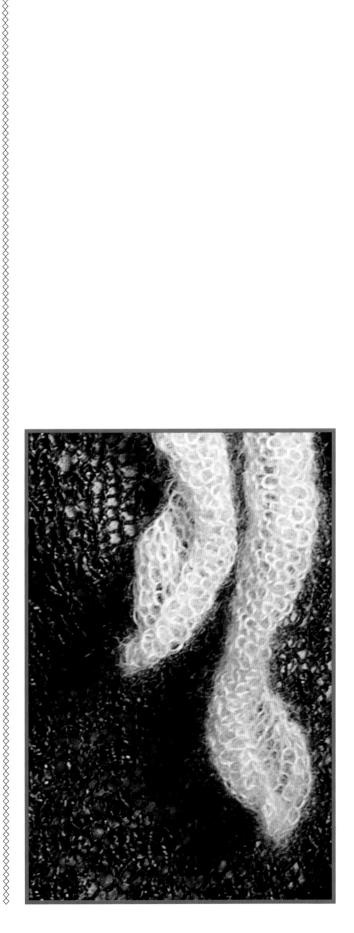

6 (7, 8) times, ridged double decrease, k to last 3 sts, skp, k1—53 (59, 65) sts.

Row 43: K8, rep from Polka Dot Lace Pattern ** 6 (7, 8) times, double increase in next st, k8—55 (61, 67) sts.

Row 45: K all sts.

BO all sts in purl.

BACK
With Yarn A and straight needles, cast on 77 (83, 89) sts.

Beg with WS row (p all sts), work in St st for 61 (65, 69) rows.

Beg Polka Dot Lace Pattern
Pattern consists of 6 sts and 4 rows.

Work in Polka Dot Lace Pattern for next 20 rows as follows:

Row 1: K19, rep from Polka Dot Lace Pattern * 6 (7, 8) times, ridged double decrease, k19 —75 (81, 87) sts.

Row 2: P all sts.

Row 3: K19, rep from Polka Dot Lace Pattern ** 6 (7, 8) times, double increase in next st, k19—77 (83, 89) sts.

Row 4: Rep row 2.

Rep rows 1–4 four more times.

ARMHOLE SHAPING
Row 1: K1, k2tog, k to center 39 (45, 51) sts, rep from Polka Dot Lace Pattern * 6 (7, 8)   times, ridged double decrease, k to last 3 sts, skp, k1.

Row 2: K1, p to last st, k1.

Row 3: K to center 39 (45, 51) sts, rep from Polka Dot Lace Pattern ** 6 (7, 8) times, double increase in next st, k to end.

Row 4: Rep row 2.

Rep rows 1–4 four more times——67 (73, 79) sts.

Work in St st for next 24 rows, dec 1 st at each side (Dec Row) of next and each 4th row as follows:

Dec Row: K1, k2tog, k to last 3 sts, skp, k1—55 (61, 67)sts.

Each even row: K1, p to last st, k1.

Next Row: K all sts.

BO all sts in purl.

FINISHING
Sew side seams.

COLLAR
With RS of front/back facing, bottom close to you, using Yarn B and crochet hook, work 37 (41, 45) overlay chs along top edge of the front and back as follows:

*Overlay ch in each of the next 2 sts in the last row, skip 1 st, rep from * to end of row.

Fasten off.

With RS of front facing, bottom close to you, using Yarn B and circular needles, CO 150 sts. Cont and pick up and k37 (41, 45) sts, inserting needle in each overlay ch of the front top, then CO 3 more sts. Cont and pick up and k37 (41, 45) sts, inserting needle in each overlay ch of the back top, then CO 150 more sts.

Beg with WS row, work in St st for next 10 rows.

BO all sts in purl.

This project was knit with

(A) 6 (7, 8) balls of Berroco Seduce Yarn, 47% rayon/25% linen/17% silk/11% nylon, medium weight, approx 1.4oz/40g = 100yd/92m per ball, color 4457

(B) 1 ball of Cascade Yarns Kid Seta Solid Yarn, 70% super kid mohair/30% silk, superfine/fingering weight, approx 0.8oz/25g = 230yds/210m, color 408

Elegant Evening Over-the-Knee Skirt

This elegant skirt is knit as a single piece, with contrasting materials for an interesting effect. Beautiful and flattering, it is very quick and easy to make. For added prettiness, it features a beautifully crocheted bottom.

EXPERIENCE LEVEL

■■■□ Intermediate

SIZES

> 36/38 (40/42, 44/46). Shown in size 36/38.

FINISHED FLAT MEASUREMENTS

> Length: 24"/61cm (25"/63.5cm, 26"/66cm)

> High waist: 14½"/37cm (16"/40cm, 17½"/44.5cm)

> Hips: 18½"/47cm (20½"/52cm, 22½"/57cm)

MATERIALS AND TOOLS

> Yarn A: **MEDIUM 4** 385yd/355m of medium weight yarn, bamboo/nylon, in variegated beige, olive green and gray

> Yarn B: **MEDIUM 4** 230yd/210m of medium weight yarn, super kid mohair/silk, in black

> Elastic thread (black)

> Size 10.75 (7mm) by 24" to 32" circular knitting needles OR SIZE TO OBTAIN GAUGE

> Size 8 (5mm) by 24" to 32" circular knitting needles OR SIZE TO OBTAIN GAUGE

> 2 stitch markers

> Size E/4 (3.5mm) crochet hook OR SIZE TO OBTAIN GAUGE

> 2 stitch markers

> Scissors

GAUGE

> With larger needles and Yarn A, in St st, 14 sts and 16 rows to 4"/10cm

> With smaller needles and Yarn A, in St st, 18 sts and 20 rows to 4"/10cm

Measurements

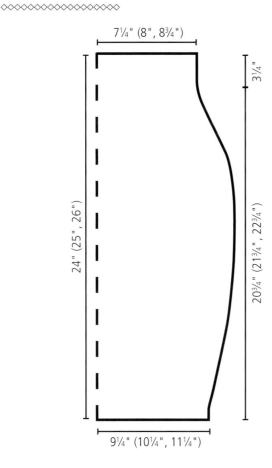

7¼" (8", 8¾")

3¼"

24" (25", 26")

20¾" (21¾", 22¾")

9¼" (10¼", 11¼")

ELONGATED STITCH PATTERN

Pattern consists of 1 st and 2 rnds.

Rnd 1: *K1, yo twice, rep from * to end of rnd.

Rnd 2: *K1, drop off 2 yarn overs, rep from * to end of rnd.

Instructions

Note Purl side is RS of this skirt.

With larger circular needles and Yarn A, cast on 130 (144, 158) sts.

Beg at bottom of skirt, work in St st (k all sts for circular knitting) for next 4 rnds, marking 1st and 65th (72nd, 79th) sts [first 65 (72, 79) sts are front and last 65 (72, 79) sts are back].

Inc Rnd: Inc 2 sts at front and 2 sts at back as follows: inc1, k to last st of front (2nd marked st), inc1 in each of next 2 sts, k to last st of back (one st before 1st marked st), inc1—134 (148, 162) sts.

Work in Elongated Stitch Pattern for next 2 rnds.

Work in St st for next 3 rnds, replacing stitch markers and marking 1st and 67th (74th, 81st) sts.

Rep Inc Rnd once—138 (152, 166) sts.

Work in Elongated Stitch Pattern for next 2 rnds.

Work in St st for next 3 rnds, replacing stitch markers and marking 1st and 69th (76th, 83rd) sts.

Rep Inc Rnd once—142 (156, 170) sts.

Work in Elongated Stitch Pattern for next 2 rnds.

Work in St st for next 3 rnds, replacing stitch markers and marking 1st and 71st (78th, 85th) sts.

Rep Inc Rnd once—146 (160, 174) sts.

Work in Elongated Stitch Pattern for next 2 rnds.

Work in St st for next 40 (44, 48) rnds, replacing stitch markers and marking 1st and 73rd (80th, 87th) sts.

Dec Rnd: Dec 2 sts at front and 2 sts at back as follows: k2tog, k to last 2 sts of front (one st before 2nd marked st), skp, k2tog, k to last 2 sts of back (two sts before 1st marked st), skp—142 (156, 170) sts.

Work in St st for next 4 rnds, replacing stitch markers and marking 1st and 71st (78th, 85th) sts.

Rep Dec Rnd once—138 (152, 166) sts.

Work in St st for next 4 rnds, replacing stitch markers and marking 1st and 69th (76th, 83rd) sts.

Rep Dec Rnd once—134 (148, 162) sts.

Work in St st for next 4 rnds, replacing stitch markers and marking 1st and 67th (74th, 81st) sts.

Rep Dec Rnd once—130 (144, 158) sts.

WAIST

Using smaller circular needles, work in St st for next 5 rnds.

Purl all sts for next 8 rnds.

BO all sts in purl.

FINISHING

Crocheted waist top
Rnd 1: With RS (purl side) of skirt facing, bottom close to you and Yarn B, insert hook in 1st bound-off st of waist, ch 1, sc in same st, sc in each of next bound-off sts all around waist. Join with sl st in 1st sc.

Rnd 2: *Ch 4, sl st in 3rd sc from hook, rep from * all around waist. Make last sl st in 1st sc of prev rnd. Fasten off.

Crocheted skirt bottom
Rnd 1: With RS of skirt facing, top close to you and Yarn B, insert hook in 1st cast-on st of skirt bottom, ch 4, *sl st in 2nd cast on st from hook, ch 3, rep from * all around skirt bottom, sl st in 1st ch.

Rnd 2: Sl st in next ch, sl st in 1st ch-4 space of prev rnd, *ch 4, sl st in next ch-3 space of prev rnd, rep from * all around skirt bottom. Make last sl st in 1st ch-4 space of prev rnd.

Rnd 3: Sl st in each of next 2 ch sts, sl st in 1st ch-4 space of prev rnd, *ch 5, sl st in next ch-4 space of prev rnd, rep from * all around skirt bottom. Make last sl st in 1st ch-5 space of prev rnd.

Rnd 4: Sl st in each of next 2 ch sts, sl st in 1st ch-5 space of prev rnd, *ch 6, sl st in next ch-5 space of prev rnd, rep from * all around skirt bottom. Make last sl st in 1st ch-6 space of prev rnd. Fasten off.

Adjusting elastic thread to waist
With RS of skirt facing, bottom close to you and elastic thread, insert hook in 1st k st of last row of skirt waist, work overlay ch in each of next k sts of this rnd. Join with overlay ch in 1st overlay ch st.

Fasten off.

Follow same instructions for adjusting elastic thread in each of next 7 top rnds of skirt waist.

This project was knit with

(A) 5 (6, 7) balls of Berroco Bonsai yarn, 97% bamboo/3% nylon, medium weight, approx 1.75oz/50g = 77yd/71m per ball, color 4196

(B) 1 ball of Cascade Yarns Kid Seta, 70% super kid mohair/30% silk, medium weight, approx 0.88oz/25g = 230yd/210m per ball, color 407

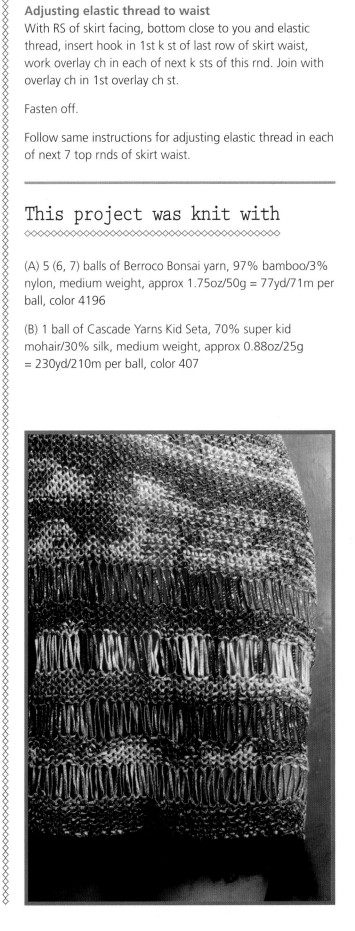

Daring Décolleté Dress

This brilliant red dress makes the traditional Little Black Dress look dull in comparison! With a low-cut front and even lower-cut back, it is simple yet seductive. Perfect for very special evenings, it's surprisingly easy to make. No sewn seams at all!

EXPERIENCE LEVEL

▬ ▬ ▬ ▭ Intermediate

SIZES

> 36 (38/40, 42/44). Shown in size 36.

FINISHED FLAT MEASUREMENTS

> Chest at underarms: 16½"/42cm (18"/46cm, 20½"/52cm)

> Length: 44"/112cm (44 ¾"/114cm, 44½"/113cm)

> Upper arms: 7½"/19cm (8"/20cm, 8½"/21.5cm)

MATERIALS AND TOOLS

> Yarn A: (MEDIUM 4) 1770yd/1620m of medium weight yarn, viscose/wool, in bright red

> Yarn B: (MEDIUM 4) 177yd/162m of medium weight yarn, viscose/wool, in deep red

> Size 8 (5mm) straight knitting needles OR SIZE TO OBTAIN GAUGE

> Size 8 (5mm) by 24" to 32" circular knitting needles OR SIZE TO OBTAIN GAUGE

> Size E/4 (3.5) crochet hook OR SIZE TO OBTAIN GAUGE

> Scissors

GAUGE

> In St st, 18 sts and 16 rows to 4"/10cm

Measurements

◇◇◇◇◇◇◇◇◇◇◇◇◇◇◇

5¾" (6¼", 6¾")

8¾" (9¼", 9¾")

6¾" (6¼", 8¼")

5½"

6" (7", 8")

13½" (13¾", 13½")

6¾" (6¾", 8¾")

17"

7½" (8", 8½")

36" (36¼", 36")

10" (11", 12")

Instructions

◇◇◇◇◇◇◇◇◇◇◇◇◇◇◇

SKIRT

With circular needles and Yarn A, cast on 180 (198, 216) sts.

Beg at bottom of dress, work in St st (k all sts for circular knitting) for next 68 rnds.

BO all sts.

TOP

With RS of skirt facing, bottom close to you, using Yarn A and circular needle, pick up and k120 (138, 156) sts all around skirt top, as follows:

*Insert needle in back lp only of each of next 2 bound-off sts of skirt (beg with 1st bound-off st), skp 1 st, rep from * 60 (66, 72) times.

*Work in St st for next 7 rnds.

Dec Rnd 1: K1, k2tog, k55 (k64, k73) skp, k1, k2tog, k55 (k64, k73), skp.

*Next Rnd (Dec Rnd): K1, k2tog, k to last st before 1st dec of prev rnd, skp, k1, k2tog, k to last st before 4th dec of prev rnd, skp.

Rep from * once more—108 (126, 144) sts.

Work in St st for next 24 rnds.

Next Rnd (Inc Rnd): K1, inc 1, k50 (k59, k68) inc 1, k2, inc 1, k50 (k59, k68), inc 1, k1—112 (130, 148) sts.

For size 40/42 only
Next Rnd (Inc Rnd): *Inc 1, k64, rep from * once more—132 sts.

For all sizes
Work in St st for next 5 (4, 5) rnds.

Transfer 28 (33, 37) sts (this will be the left half of back) from left needle to right needle.

Beg Back Décolleté
Beginning at center of back, using straight needles and Yarn A, work next rows as follows:

Row 1 (Inc Row): K26 (k31, k35), inc 1, k2, inc 1, k52 (62, 70), inc 1, k2, inc 1, k26 (k31, k35)—116 (136, 152) sts.

Row 2 and each even row: K1, p to last st, k1.

Work in St st for next 4 rows.

Next Row (Inc Row): K27 (k32, k36), inc 1, k2, inc 1, k54 (64, 72), inc 1, k2, inc 1, k27 (k32, k36)—120 (140, 156) sts.

LEFT BACK AND FRONT HALF
Beg Front Décolleté
Row 1: K60 (k70, k78). Transfer 60 (70, 78) sts of right front and back onto stitch holder.

Row 2 and each even row: K1, p to last st, k1.

Work in St st for next 12 rows.

Left back armhole and shoulder shaping
Row 1: K30 (k35, k39). Transfer 30 (k35, k39) sts of left front onto stitch holder.

Row 2: BO 4 sts in purl, p to last st, k1—26 (31, 35) sts.

For size 40/42 (44/46) only
Row 3: K all sts.

Row 4: BO 3 sts in purl, p to last st, k1—28 (32) sts.

For size 44/46 only
Row 5: K all sts.

Row 6: BO 2 sts in purl, p to last st, k1—30 sts.

For all sizes
Work in St st for next 28 rows.

Short rows
Row 31: K9 (k9, k10), wrap and turn.

Row 32: Work back the other way, p to last st, k1.

Row 33: K to wrapped st, k the wrap and st tog, k8 (k8, k9), wrap and turn.

Row 34: Work back the other way, p to last st, k1.

Row 35: K to wrapped st, k the wrap and st tog, k to end.

BO all sts in purl.

Left front armhole and shoulder shaping
Transfer 30 (35, 39) sts of left front back to a straight knitting needle.

Work to correspond to left back, reversing shaping.

Work wrap and turn of short rows on purl side.

RIGHT BACK AND FRONT HALF
Transfer 60 (70, 78) sts of right back and front half back to a straight knitting needle.

Work to correspond to left back and front half until armhole and shoulder shaping.

Right front armhole and shoulder shaping
Work to correspond to left back armhole and shoulder.

Right back armhole and shoulder shaping
Work to correspond to left front armhole and shoulder.

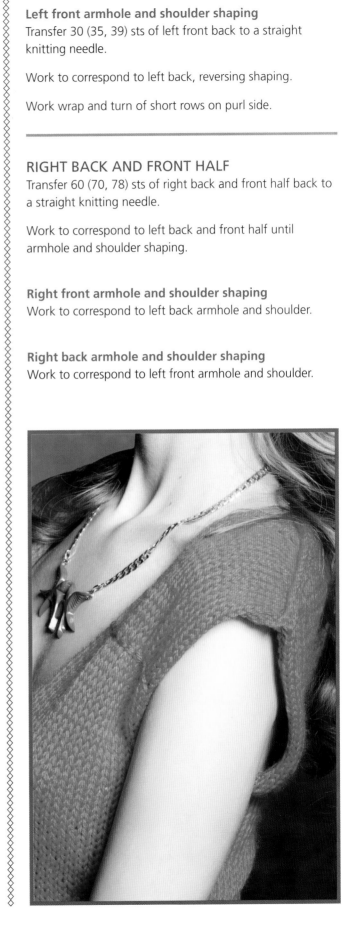

55

FINISHING

Crocheting right/left armhole border

With RS of front/back facing, bottom to your left, using Yarn B and crochet hook, work overlay chs all around right/left armhole, inserting hook in each row space between the 1st and 2nd sts. Fasten off.

Right/Left front half gather

With RS of front facing, bottom close to you, using Yarn B and crochet hook, work 13 (14, 15) overlay chs across right/left front half of the dress, inserting hook in every other st of 12th armholes row. Fasten off.

Crocheting neckline

With RS of front/back facing bottom to your left, using Yarn B and crochet hook, work overlay chs all along front/back neckline, inserting hook in each row space between the 1st and 2nd sts. Fasten off.

Shoulder seams

With RS of front facing, bottom close to you, using Yarn B and crochet hook, work 17 (18, 19) overlay chs along front left/right shoulders as follows:

Insert hook in last row 1st st of front left/right shoulder and its corresponding st at back left/right shoulder, *work overlay ch in each of next 2 sts of front left/right shoulder and its corresponding sts at back left/right shoulder, skp 1, rep from * all along last row of front left/right shoulder. Fasten off. Rep on other shoulder.

Crocheting skirt/top junction

With RS of dress facing, top close to you, using Yarn B and crochet hook, work overlay chs all around skirt and top junction, inserting hook in each unused lp of the bound-off sts of the skirt. Fasten off.

Faux plisse fold

With RS of front/back facing bottom to your left, using Yarn B and crochet hook, work 20 (22, 24) faux plisse folds as follows:

1st plisse fold

Insert hook under left leg of leftmost st at last rnd of skirt and under right leg of next st same rnd, work overlay chs from top of skirt to bottom, inserting hook under left legs of leftmost sts of each rnd, and under right legs of corresponding sts. Fasten off.

Next plisse fold

*Insert hook under left leg of 8th st from prev plisse fold at last rnd of skirt and under right leg of next st same rnd, work overlay chs from top of skirt to bottom, inserting hook under left legs of 8th st of each rnd and under right legs of corresponding sts. Fasten off.

Rep from * 19 times.

Bottom border

With WS of dress facing, top close to you, using Yarn B and crochet hook, work overlay chs all around dress bottom, inserting hook in each CO st. Fasten off.

With WS of dress facing, top close to you, using Yarn B and circular needles, pick up and k all around dress bottom, inserting needle in front lp only of each overlay ch.

Rnd 1: P all sts.

BO all sts in purl.

This project was knit with

(A) 10 (11, 12) balls of Stitch Nation Bamboo Ewe Yarn, 55% viscose/45% wool, medium weight, approx 3.5oz/100g + 177yd/162m per ball, color 5280

(B) 1 ball of Stitch Nation Bamboo Ewe Yarn, 55% viscose/45% wool, medium weight, approx 3.5oz/100g = 177yd/162m per ball, color 5910

Incredible Cable Sweater

This modern design features cable knits at the front and on the forearms. Shaped with body-hugging loose ribbing, it's stylishly urban and very warm. Note that the wide cowl neck is knit as part of the sweater, rather than sewn on, for a modern look.

EXPERIENCE LEVEL

 Intermediate

SIZES

> 36 (38/40, 42/44). Shown in size 38/40.

FINISHED FLAT MEASUREMENTS

> Chest at underarms: 16½"/42cm (19"/48cm, 21½"/55cm)

> Length: 24"/61cm (24"/61cm, 26¾"/68cm)

> Upper arms: 8"/20cm (8"/20cm, 8¾"/22cm)

MATERIALS AND TOOLS

> 1,441yd/1331m of medium weight yarn, wool/alpaca, in dark purple

> Size 8 (5mm) straight knitting needles OR SIZE TO OBTAIN GAUGE

> Size 8 (5mm) by 24" to 32" circular knitting needles OR SIZE TO OBTAIN GAUGE

> Cable needle

> Stitch holder

> Yarn needle

> Scissors

GAUGE

> In St st, 18 sts and 26 rows to 4"/10cm

Measurements

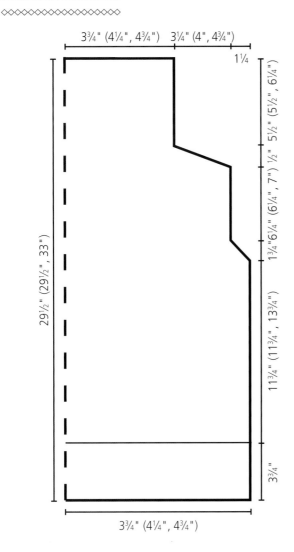

3¾" (4¼", 4¾")   3¼" (4", 4¾")

1¼

5½" (5½", 6¼")

½"

6¼" (6¼", 7")

1¾"

11¾" (11¾", 13¾")

29½" (29½", 33")

3¾"

3¾" (4¼", 4¾")

CABLE PATTERN

Pattern consists of 33 sts and 8 rows

Cable Twist-Crossing to the Left Using 18 stitches (C18F)

Sl next 9 sts onto cable needle and hold at front of work, k next 9 sts, slip 9 stitches from cable needle back to left needle, k these stitches.

Cable Twist-Crossing to the Left Using 18 stitches (C18B)

Sl next 9 sts onto cable needle and hold at back of work, k next 9 sts, slip 9 stitches from cable needle back to left needle, k these stitches.

Instructions

FRONT

With straight needles, cast on 91 (103, 115) sts.

Work in rib pattern for next 24 rows as follows: k2, (p3, k3) 14 (16, 18) times, p3, k2.

Work in St st for 44 (44, 56) rows.

Beg Cable Pattern

Pattern consists of 33 sts and 8 rows.

Work in Cable Pattern for next 32 rows as follows:

Row 1: Beg at RS row, k29 (k35, k41) sts, work (p3, k27, p3) on 33 center sts, k to end.

Row 2: P29 (p35, p41) sts, work (k3, p27, k3) on 33 center sts, p to end.

Rep rows 1–2 four more times.

Cable Twist Row (crossing to left): K29 (k35, k41) sts, (p3 sts, C18F, k9, p3 sts), k to end.

Rep row 2.

Rep rows 1–2 four more times.

Cable Twist Row (crossing to right): k29 (k35, k41) sts, (p3 sts, k9, C18B, p3 sts), k to end.

Rep row 2.

Rep rows 1–2 four more times.

Rep Cable Twist Row (crossing to left).

Rep row 2.

Armhole shaping

Dec 1 st at each side every other row 6 times as follows:

Row 1: K1, k2tog, k to cable panel, work (p3, k27, p3) on 33 center sts, k to last 3 sts, skp, k1.

Row 2: P to cable panel, work (k3, p27, k3) on 33 center sts, p to end.

Rep rows 1–2 three more times.

Cable Twist Row (crossing to right): K1, k2tog, k to cable panel, (p3 sts, k9, C18B, p3 sts), k to last 3 sts, skp, k1.

Rep row 2.

Rep rows 1–2 one more time—79 (91, 103) sts.

Armhole ribbing
Work next rows as follows:

Row 1: Work in (k2, p2) rib pattern twice, k to cable panel, work (p3, k27, p3) on 33 center sts, k to last 8 sts, work in (p2, k2) rib pattern to end.

Row 2: K the knits and p the purls.

Rep row 1 and row 2 two more times.

Cable Twist Row (crossing to left): Work in (k2, p2) rib pattern twice, (p3 sts, C18F, k9, p3 sts), k to last 8 sts, work in (p2, k2) rib pattern to end.

Rep row 2.

Rep rows 1–2 four more times.

Cable Twist Row (crossing to right): Work in (k2, p2) rib pattern twice, (p3 sts, k9, C18B, p3 sts), k to last 8 sts, work in (k2, p2) rib pattern to end.

Rep row 2

Rep rows 1–2 five more times

*Next Row: Work in (k2, p2) rib pattern twice, k to last 8 sts, work in (p2, k2) rib pattern to end.

Rep row 2.

Rep from * 3 (3, 5) more times.

Shoulder shaping and wide cowl neck
BO 5 (6, 7) sts from each side each row 3 times as follows:

Row 1: BO in k first 5 (6, 7) sts, k to center 45 (51, 57) sts, for wide rib cowl neck work (p3, k3) rib 7 (8, 9) times, p3, k to end.

Row 2: BO in purl first 5 (6, 7) sts, k the knits and p the purls.

Rep rows 1–2 two more times—49 (55, 61) sts.

Transfer rem 49 (55, 61) sts for wide polo neck onto stitch holder.

BACK
Work same as for front until Cable Pattern of front begins.

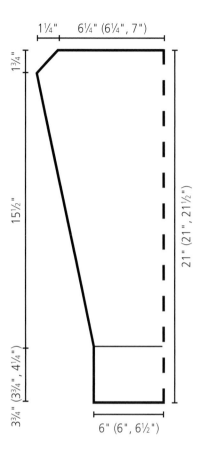

1¼"   6¼" (6¼", 7")

1¾"

15½"

3¾" (3¾", 4¼")

21" (21", 21½")

6" (6", 6½")

Work next 32 rows as follows:

Row 1: Beg at RS row, k23 (k26, k29) sts, on 45 (51, 57) center sts work (p3, k3) rib 7 (8, 9) times, p3, k to end.

Row 2: K the knits and p the purls.

Rep rows 1–2 fifteen more times.

Armhole shaping
Dec 1 st at each side every other row 6 times as follows:

Row 1: K1, k2tog, k to center 45 (51, 57) sts, work (p3, k3) rib 7 (8, 9) times, p3, k to last 3 sts, skp, k1.

Row 2: K the knits and p the purls.

Rep rows 1–2 five more times—79 (91, 103) sts.

Armhole ribbing
*Next Row: Work in (k2, p2) rib pattern twice, k to center 45 (51, 57) sts, work (p3, k3) rib 7 (8, 9) times, p3, k to last 8 sts, work in (p2, k2) rib pattern to end.

Row 2: K the knits and p the purls. Rep from * 17 (17, 19) more times

Shoulder shaping and wide cowl neck
Work same as for front.

SLEEVES (MAKE TWO)
With straight needles, cast on 55 (55, 59) sts.

Work in rib pattern for next 24 (24, 28) rows as follows: k2 (k2, k4), (p3, k3) rib 8 times, p3, k2 (k2, k4).

Work in St st for next 98 rows, beg Cable Pattern from 67th row and inc 1 st at each side (Inc Row) of 1st, 15th, 29th, 43rd, 53rd, 63rd , 73rd, 81st, 89th and 97th rows, as follows:

Inc Row: K1, inc 1, k to last 2 sts, inc 1, k1.

Beg Cable Pattern
Pattern consists of 33 sts and 8 rows.

Row 67: Beg at RS row, k to center 33 sts, work (p3, k27, p3) on 33 center sts, k to end.

Row 68: K the knits and p the purls.

Rep row 67 and row 68 four more times.

Cable Twist Row (crossing to left): K to center 33 sts, (p3 sts, C18F, k9, p3 sts), k to end.

Rep row 68.

Rep rows 67–68 four more times.

Cable Twist Row (crossing to right): K to center 33 sts, (p3 sts, k9, C18B, p3 sts), k to end.

Rep row 68.

Rep rows 67–68 five more times—75 (75, 79) sts and 98 rows.

Sleeve top shaping
Dec 1 st at each side of every other row 6 times as follows:

Row 1: K1, k2tog, k to last 3 sts, skp, k1.

Row 2: P all sts.

Rep row 1 and row 2 five more times—63 (63, 67) sts.

BO all sts.

WIDE COWL NECK
Transfer all rem sts of front and back from stitch holders onto circular needles—98 (110, 122) sts.

Work in rib pattern for next 36 (36, 40) rnds as follows: *[k2, (p3, k3) rib 7 (8, 9) times, p3, k2], rep from * once more.

BO all sts in rib pattern.

FINISHING
Sew shoulder seams.

Set in sleeves sewing bound-off sts at top of sleeve to bound-off armhole sts.

Sew side seams.

This project was knit with

10 (11, 12) balls of Stitch Nation Alpaca Love, medium weight, 80%wool/20%alpaca, approx 3oz/85g = 131yd/ 121m per ball, color 3580

Wavy Wonders A-Line Skirt

In this below-the-knee skirt, yarns of different colors are knit together in a wave pattern, creating a visual fabric that is eye-catching and distinct. The skirt requires minimal shaping, but the result is both stylish and interesting.

EXPERIENCE LEVEL

■■■□ Intermediate

SIZES

> 36/38 (40/42, 44/46). Shown in size 36/38.

FINISHED FLAT MEASUREMENTS

> Length with folded waist: 30"/76cm
> Waist: 14½"/36cm (16½"/42cm, 19"/48cm)

MATERIALS AND TOOLS

> Yarn A: **BULKY 5** 240yd/218m of chunky weight yarn, acrylic/wool, in cobalt blue
> Yarn B: **BULKY 5** 240yd/218m of chunky weight yarn, acrylic/wool, in dark gray
> Yarn C: **BULKY 5** 120yd/109m of chunky weight yarn, acrylic/wool, in light gray
> Yarn D: **BULKY 5** 120yd/109m of chunky weight yarn, acrylic/wool, in reddish purple
> Yarn E: **BULKY 5** 120yd/109m of chunky weight yarn, acrylic/wool, in bright pink
> Size 11 (8mm) by 24" to 32" circular knitting needles OR SIZE TO OBTAIN GAUGE
> Scissors

GAUGE

> In St st, 11 sts and 15 rows to 4"/10cm

Measurements

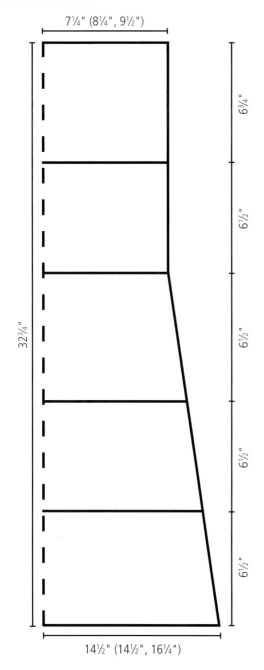

7¼" (8¼", 9½")

6¾"

6½"

6½"

6½"

6½"

32¾"

14½" (14½", 16¼")

ELONGATED STITCH WAVE PATTERN

Pattern consists of 20 sts and 4 rnds.

Rnd 1: *K5, (yo once, k1) 3 times, (yo twice, k1) 4 times, (yo once, k1) 3 times, k5, rep from * to end of rnd (or as indicated).

Rnd 2: *K5, (drop off 1 yarn over, k1) 3 times, (drop

off 2 yarn overs, k1) 4 times, (drop off 1 yarn over, k1) 3 times, k5, rep from * to end of rnd (or as indicated).

Rnd 3: *(yo twice, k1) twice, (yo once, k1) 3 times, k10, (yo once, k1) 3 times, (yo twice, k1) twice, rep from * to end of rnd (or as indicated).

Rnd 4: *(drop off 2 yarn overs, k1) twice, (drop off 1 yarn over, k1) 3 times, k10, (drop off 1 yarn over, k1) 3 times, (drop off 2 yarn overs, k1) twice, rep from * to end of rnd (or as indicated).

Instructions

BOTTOM LAYER

With circular needles and Yarn C, cast on 160 (160, 180) sts.

Rnd 1: Beg at bottom of skirt, work in St st (k all sts for circular knitting) for 1 rnd. Cut Yarn C.

Rnd 2: Join Yarn B, work rnd 1 of Elongated Stitch Wave Pattern, rep from * 8 (8, 9) times. Cut Yarn B.

Rnd 3: Join Yarn E, work rnd 2 of Elongated Stitch Wave Pattern, rep from * 8 (8, 9) times. Cut Yarn E.

Rnd 4: Join Yarn A, work rnd 3 of Elongated Stitch Wave Pattern, rep from * 8 (8, 9) times. Cut Yarn A.

Rnd 5: Join Yarn E, work rnd 4 of Elongated Stitch Wave Pattern, rep from * 8 (8, 9) times. Cut Yarn E.

Rnd 6: Rep rnd 2.

Rnd 7: Join Yarn C, work rnd 2 of Elongated Stitch Wave Pattern, rep from * 8 (8, 9) times.

Rnds 8–9: K all sts. Cut Yarn C.

Rnd 10: Join Yarn B, work rnd 3 of Elongated Stitch Wave Pattern, rep from * 8 (8, 9) times. Cut Yarn B.

Rnd 11: Join Yarn D, work rnd 4 of Elongated Stitch Wave Pattern, rep from * 8 (8, 9) times. Cut Yarn D.

Rnd 12: Join Yarn A, work rnd 1 of Elongated Stitch Wave Pattern, rep from * 8 (8, 9) times. Cut Yarn A.

Rnd 13: Join Yarn D, work rnd 2 of Elongated Stitch Wave Pattern, rep from * 8 (8, 9) times. Cut Yarn D.

Rnd 14: Rep rnd 10.

Rnd 15: Join Yarn C, work rnd 4 of Elongated Stitch Wave Pattern, rep from * 8 (8, 9) times.

Rnds 16–17: Rep rnds 8–9.

Rnds 18–25: Rep rnds 2–9.

BO all sts loosely.

MIDDLE LAYER

With RS of Bottom Layer facing, bottom close to you, Yarn A and circular needle, pick up and k140 (k140, k160) sts along the top edge of the Bottom Layer as follows:

*Insert needle from behind in each of next 7 (7, 8) sts in the second to last row of Bottom Layer (beg with 1st st of this row), skip 1 st, rep from * 20 times.

Rnd 1: K all sts. Cut Yarn A.

Rnd 2: Join Yarn C, work rnd 1 of Elongated Stitch Wave Pattern, rep from * 7 (7, 8) times. Cut Yarn C.

Rnd 3: Join Yarn D, work rnd 2 of Elongated Stitch Wave Pattern, rep from * 7 (7, 8) times. Cut Yarn D.

Rnd 4: Join Yarn B, work rnd 3 of Elongated Stitch Wave Pattern, rep from * 7 (7, 8) times. Cut Yarn B.

Rnd 5: Join Yarn D, work rnd 4 of Elongated Stitch Wave Pattern, rep from * 7 (7, 8) times. Cut Yarn D.

Rnd 6: Rep rnd 2.

Rnd 7: Join Yarn A, work rnd 2 of Elongated Stitch Wave Pattern, rep from * 7 (7, 8) times.

Rnds 8–9: K all sts. Cut Yarn A.

Rnd 10: Join Yarn B, work rnd 3 of Elongated Stitch Wave Pattern, rep from * 7 (7, 8) times. Cut Yarn B.

Rnd 11: Join Yarn E, work rnd 4 of Elongated Stitch Wave Pattern, rep from * 7 (7, 8) times. Cut Yarn E.

Rnd 12: Join Yarn C, work rnd 1 of Elongated Stitch Wave Pattern, rep from * 7 (7, 8) times. Cut Yarn C.

Rnd 13: Join Yarn E, work rnd 2 of Elongated Stitch Wave Pattern, rep from * 7 (7, 8) times. Cut Yarn E.

Rnd 14: Rep rnd 10.

Rnd 15: Join Yarn A, work rnd 4 of Elongated Stitch Wave Pattern, rep from * 7 (7, 8) times.

Rnds 16–17: Rep rnds 8–9.

Rnds 18–25: Rep rnds 2–9.

BO all sts loosely.

TOP LAYER

With RS of Middle Layer facing, skirt bottom close to you, Yarn B and circular needle, pick up and k120 (k120, k140) sts along the top edge of the Middle Layer as follows:

*Insert needle from behind in each of next 6 (6, 7) sts in the second to last row of the Middle Layer (beg with 1st st of this row), skip 1 st, rep from * 20 times.

Rnd 1: K all sts. Cut Yarn B.

Rnd 2: Join Yarn A, work rnd 1 of Elongated Stitch Wave Pattern, rep from * 6 (6, 7) times. Cut Yarn A.

Rnd 3: Join Yarn E, work rnd 2 of Elongated Stitch Wave Pattern, rep from * 6 (6, 7) times. Cut Yarn E.

Rnd 4: Join Yarn C, work rnd 3 of Elongated Stitch Wave Pattern, rep from * 6 (6, 7) times. Cut Yarn C.

Rnd 5: Join Yarn E, work rnd 4 of Elongated Stitch Wave Pattern, rep from * 6 (6, 7) times. Cut Yarn E.

Rnd 6: Rep rnd 2.

Rnd 7: Join Yarn B, work rnd 2 of Elongated Stitch Wave Pattern, rep from * 6 (6, 7) times.

Rnds 8–9: K all sts. Cut Yarn B.

Rnd 10: Join Yarn C, work rnd 3 of Elongated Stitch Wave Pattern, rep from * 6 (6, 7) times. Cut Yarn C.

Rnd 11: Join Yarn D, work rnd 4 of Elongated Stitch Wave Pattern, rep from * 6 (6, 7) times. Cut Yarn D.

Rnd 12: Join Yarn A, work rnd 1 of Elongated Stitch Wave Pattern, rep from * 6 (6, 7) times. Cut Yarn A.

Rnd 13: Join Yarn D, work rnd 2 of Elongated Stitch Wave Pattern, rep from * 6 (6, 7) times. Cut Yarn D.

Rnd 14: Rep rnd 10.

Rnd 15: Join Yarn B, work rnd 4 of Elongated Stitch Wave Pattern, rep from * 6 (6, 7) times.

Rnds 16–17: Rep rnds 8–9.

Rnds 18–25: Rep rnds 2–9.

BO all sts loosely.

BENT WAIST

With RS of Top Layer facing, skirt bottom close to you, Yarn A and circular needle, pick up and k80 (k90, k105) sts along top edge of the Top Layer as follows:

*Insert needle from behind in each of next 2 (3, 3) sts in the second to last row of the Middle Layer (beg with 1st st of this row), skip 1 st, rep from * 40 (30, 35) times.

Work in St st (k all sts for circular knitting) for next 25 rnds. Cut Yarn A.

Join Yarn B and work in (k4, p4) rib pattern for next 26 rnds.

BO all sts in rib pattern.

This project was knit with

(A) 2 (3, 3) balls of Bernat Roving Yarn, chunky weight, 80% acrylic/20% wool, approx 3.5oz/100g = 120yd/109m per ball, color 00104

(B) 2 (3, 3) balls of Bernat Roving Yarn, chunky weight, 80% acrylic/20% wool, approx 3.5oz/100g = 120yd/109m per ball, color 00033

(C) 1 ball of Bernat Roving Yarn, chunky weight, 80% acrylic/20% wool, approx 3.5oz/100g = 120yd/109m per ball, color 00032

(D) 1 ball of Bernat Roving Yarn, chunky weight, 80% acrylic/20% wool, approx 3.5oz/100g = 120yd/109m per ball, color 00067

(E) 1 ball of Bernat Roving Yarn, chunky weight, 80% acrylic/20% wool, approx 3.5oz/100g = 120yd/109m per ball, color 00402

Chic Shoulder Cowl

Dress up a simple outfit with this unique tweed textured cowl. Easy to make and a pleasure to wear, it upgrades every outfit while keeping you warm. Young and trendy, the texture is a tad traditional. Match it perfectly with the Fashionable Fingerless Gloves (page 73).

EXPERIENCE LEVEL

■■■□□▷ Easy

SIZES

> 36/38/40 (42/44/46). Shown in size 36/38/40.

FINISHED FLAT MEASUREMENTS

> Length: 15"/38.5cm
> Width at top: 12¼"/31cm (13¼"/34cm)
> Width at bottom: 19"/48cm (21¼"/54cm)

MATERIALS AND TOOLS

> Yarn A: **4** 650yd/595m of worsted weight yarn, wool/superkid mohair/angora, in variegated dark blue

> Yarn B: **4** 260yd/238m of worsted weight yarn, wool/superkid mohair/angora, in variegated dark purple

> Size 8 (5mm) by 24" to 32" circular knitting needles OR SIZE TO OBTAIN GAUGE

> Scissors

GAUGE

> In St st, 18 sts and 24 rows to 4"/10cm

Instructions

◇◇◇◇◇◇◇◇◇◇◇◇◇◇◇◇◇◇

COWL

Note Side with most purls is RS of this garment.

With circular needles and Yarn A, cast on 110 (120) sts.

Beg from top to bottom, work in rnds as follows:

Rnds 1–3: Work in knit (k all sts) for 3 rnds. Cut Yarn A.

Rnd 4: Join Yarn B, p all sts. Cut Yarn B.

Rnd 5: Join Yarn A, p all sts.

Rep rnds 1–5 six more times.

Rnd 36 (Inc Rnd): *K10 (k9), inc 1, rep from * 10 (12) times—120 (132) sts.

Rnds 37–39: Work in knit (k all sts) for 3 rnds. Cut Yarn A.

Rnd 40: Join Yarn B, p all sts. Cut Yarn B.

Rnd 41: Join Yarn A, p all sts.

Rnds 42–45: Work in knit (k all sts) for 4 rnds. Cut Yarn A.

Rnd 46: Join Yarn B, p all sts. Cut Yarn B.

Rnd 47: Join Yarn A, p all sts.

Rep rnds 42–47 once more.

Rnd 54 (Inc Rnd): *K11 (k10), inc 1, rep from * 10 (12) times—130 (144) sts.

Rep rnds 37–47 one more time.

Rnd 66 (Inc Rnd): *K12 (k11), inc 1, rep from * 10 (12) times—140 (156) sts.

Rnds 67–70: Work in knit (k all sts) for 4 rnds. Cut Yarn A.

Rnd 71: Join Yarn B, p all sts. Cut Yarn B.

Rnd 72: Join Yarn A, p all sts.

Rnds 73–77: Work in knit (k all sts) for 5 rnds. Cut Yarn A.

Rnd 78: Join Yarn B, p all sts. Cut Yarn B.

Rnd 79: Join Yarn A, p all sts.

Rep rnds 73–77 two more times.

Rnd 90 (Inc Rnd): *K13 (k12), inc 1, rep from * 10 (12) times—150 (168) sts.

Rnds 91–95: Work in knit (k all sts) for 5 rnds. Cut Yarn A.

Rnd 96: Join Yarn B, p all sts. Cut Yarn B.

Rnd 97: Join Yarn A, p all sts.

Rnd 98 (Inc Rnd): *K14 (k13), inc 1, rep from * 10 (12) times—160 (180) sts.

Rep rnds 91–97 one more time.

Rnd 106 (Inc Rnd): *K15 (k14), inc 1, rep from * 10 (12) times—170 (192) sts.

Rnds 107–112: Work in knit (k all sts) for 6 rnds.

BO all sts.

This project was knit with

◇◇◇◇◇◇◇◇◇◇◇◇◇◇◇◇◇◇◇◇◇◇◇◇◇◇◇◇◇◇◇◇◇

(A) 5 (6, 6) balls of Berroco Blackstone Tweed Yarn, 65% wool/25% superkid mohair/10% angora, worsted weight, approx 1.75oz/50g = 130yd/119m per ball, color 2616

(B) 2 balls of Berroco Blackstone Tweed Yarn, 65% wool/25% superkid mohair/10% angora, worsted weight, approx 1.75oz/50g = 130yd/119m per ball, color 2636

Fashionable Fingerless Gloves

Dramatic on their own, these gloves make a fantastic set with the Chic Shoulder Cowl (page 71).
Easy-to-knit, practical and one-size-fits-all, they make great gifts. Make sure to make yourself a pair too!

EXPERIENCE LEVEL

Easy

SIZES

> One size

FINISHED FLAT MEASUREMENTS

> Length: 17½"/44.5cm
> Maximum width: 5½"/14cm

MATERIALS AND TOOLS

> Yarn A: 260yd/238m of worsted weight yarn,
wool/superkid mohair/angora, in variegated dark blue
> Yarn B: 130yd/119m of worsted weight yarn,
wool/superkid mohair/angora, in variegated dark purple
> Size 8 (5mm) straight knitting needles OR SIZE TO
OBTAIN GAUGE
> Scissors
> Yarn needle

GAUGE

> In St st, 18 sts and 24 rows to 4"/10cm

Instructions

RIGHT/LEFT GLOVE (MAKE TWO)

Note Purl side is RS of these gloves.

With Yarn B, cast on 38 sts.

Beg at bottom of right/left glove, work in rib pattern for next 3 rows as follows: k3, (p2, k2) 8 times, p3. Cut Yarn B.

Rows 1–2: Join Yarn A. Work in knit (k all sts) for 2 rows.

Rows 3–4: Work in St st for 2 rows, beg with purl row. Cut Yarn A.

Row 5: Join Yarn B, work in knit (k all sts) for one more row. Cut Yarn B.

Rows 6–7: Join Yarn A. Work in purl (p all sts) for 2 rows.

Rows 8–9: Work in St st for 2 rows, beg with knit row. Cut Yarn A.

Row 10: Join Yarn B, work in purl (p all sts) for one more row. Cut Yarn B.

Rep rows 1–10 two more times.

Rep rows 1–5 once more.

Rows 36–37: Join Yarn A. Work in purl (p all sts) for 2 rows.

Rows 38–40: Work in St st for 3 rows, beg with knit row. Cut Yarn A.

Row 41: Join Yarn B, work in knit (k all sts) for one more row. Cut Yarn B.

Rep rows 36–41 four more times.

Rows 65–66: Join Yarn A. Work in purl (p all sts) for 2 rows.

Row 67 (Inc Row): K1, inc 1, k to last 2 sts, inc 1, k1— 40 sts.

Rows 68–70: Work in St st for 3 rows, beg with purl row. Cut Yarn A.

Row 71: Join Yarn B, work in purl (p all sts) for one more row. Cut Yarn B.

Rows 72–73: Join Yarn A. Work in knit (k all sts) for 2 rows.

Rows 74–77: Work in St st for 4 rows, beg with purl row. Cut Yarn A.

Row 78: Join Yarn B, work in knit (k all sts) for one more row. Cut Yarn B.

Rows 79–80: Join Yarn A. Work in purl (p all sts) for 2 rows.

Rows 81–84: Work in St st for 4 rows, beg with knit row. Cut Yarn A.

Row 85: Join Yarn B, work in purl (p all sts) for one more row. Cut Yarn B.

Row 86: Join Yarn A. Work in knit (k all sts) for 1 row.

Row 87 (Inc Row): K1, inc 1, k to last 2 sts, inc 1, k1—42 sts.

Rows 88–92: Work in St st for 5 rows, beg with purl row. Cut Yarn A.

Row 93: Join Yarn B, work in purl (p all sts) for one more row. Cut Yarn B.

Rows 94–95: Join Yarn A. Work in knit (k all sts) for 2 rows.

Rep rows 88–93 once more.

Row 102: Join Yarn A. Work in knit (k all sts) for 1 row.

Row 103 (Inc Row): K1, inc 1, k to last 2 sts, inc 1, k1—44 sts.

Rows 104–109: Work in St st for 6 rows, beg with purl row.

BO all sts.

RIGHT/LEFT THUMB

With RS (mostly purl side) of right/left glove facing, bottom to your right and Yarn B, beg 3"/7.5cm to the left of glove bottom, pick up and k9 sts along glove edge from bottom to top, inserting needle in the 2nd st of each row. Don't cut yarn. Place glove bottom to your left, cont and pick up and k9 sts along other glove edge, from top to bottom, inserting needle in the 2nd st of each row—18 sts.

Work in rib pattern for next 2 rows, beg at WS row, as follows: (p2, k2) 4 times, p2.

K the knits and P the purls on RS.

BO all sts in rib pattern.

FINISHING

With WS (mostly knit side) of right/left glove facing, bottom to your right, and folding glove in half vertically, sew long sides together, making a seam from glove bottom to thumb top, and then from thumb bottom to glove top.

This project was knit with

(A) 2 balls of Berroco Blackstone Tweed Yarn, 65% wool/25% superkid mohair/10% angora, worsted weight, approx 1.75oz/50g = 130yd/119m per ball, color 2616

(B) 1 ball of Berroco Blackstone Tweed Yarn, 65% wool/25% superkid mohair/10% angora, worsted weight, approx 1.75oz/50g = 130yd/119m per ball, color 2636

Fabulously Flared Pompom Skirt

This playful design is inspired by a love of the 1950s and a passion for knit designs. It features handmade pompoms and a playful diamond pattern. As for the shape, it is made by interspersing flared godet pleats with straight pleats, creating a look that is fantastically fun!

EXPERIENCE LEVEL

■■■□ Intermediate

SIZES

> 36/38 (40/42, 44/46). Shown in size 36/38.

FINISHED FLAT MEASUREMENTS

> Length: 24"/61cm

> High waist (maximum): 15"/38.5cm (16½"/42cm, 18½"/47cm)

MATERIALS AND TOOLS

> Yarn A: **MEDIUM 4** 400m/435yds of medium weight yarn, viscose/wool, in dark blue

> Yarn B: **MEDIUM 4** 400m/435yds of medium weight yarn, viscose/wool, in green

> Yarn C: **MEDIUM 4** 80m/87yds of medium weight yarn, viscose/wool, in brown

> Size 8 (5mm) straight knitting needles OR SIZE TO OBTAIN GAUGE

> Size 8 (5mm) by 24" to 32" circular knitting needles OR SIZE TO OBTAIN GAUGE

> Size E/4 (3.5) crochet hook OR SIZE TO OBTAIN GAUGE

> Safety pin

> Tracing paper, pencil, and permanent marker

> Scissors

> Large piece of cardboard

> Yarn needle

GAUGE

> In St st, 15 sts and 24 rows to 4"/10cm

Measurements

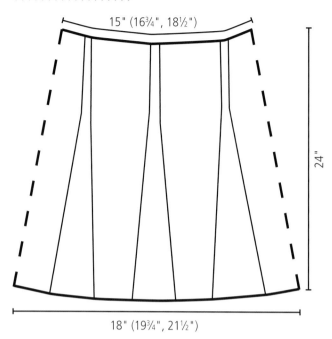

15" (16¾", 18½")

24"

18" (19¾", 21½")

DIAMOND PATTERN

Pattern consists of 6 sts and 7 rows

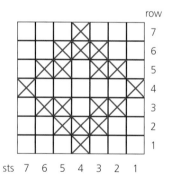

row

7
6
5
4
3
2
1

sts 7 6 5 4 3 2 1

Color and stitch key

With Yarn A [A, B], K on RS rows and P on WS rows: ☐

With Yarn B [C, A], K on RS rows and P on WS rows: ☒

Instructions

Note This skirt was knit vertically, beginning from the side seams.

FRONT
Straight pleat 1

With crochet hook and Yarn A, loosely ch 90 sts.

With straight needles, pick up and k90 sts, inserting needle in each ch st.

Beg with WS row, work in St st for 3 rows.

Beg Diamond Pattern

Beg with RS row and Yarn A, work 2 sts in St st, join Yarn B and work in Diamond Pattern, rep pattern 14 times over 85 sts (to complete last diamond, work st 7 of Diamond Pattern). Cont with Yarn A, work 3 last sts in St st.

Cont as established for 7 rows.

Beg with WS row and Yarn A, work in St st for 6 (8, 10) more rows.

Godet Pleat 1
Short rows

Row 1 (WS): P8, wrap and turn.

Row 2: Work back the other way, k8.

Row 3: P to wrapped st, p the wrap and st tog, p7, wrap and turn.

Row 4: Work back the other way, k to end.

Rep rows 3–4 two more times.

Rep row 3 one more time.

Beg Diamond Pattern

Row 10: K50 with Yarn C and work row 1 of Diamond Pattern on 37 sts, rep pattern 6 times, cont with Yarn A, k3.

Row 11: P3, with Yarn C, work row 2 of Diamond Pattern on 37 sts, rep pattern 6 times, with Yarn A, p to wrapped st, p the wrap and st tog, p7, wrap and turn.

Rows 12–15: Rep rows 10–11 two more times, working rows 3–6 of Diamond Pattern on 37 sts.

Rep row 10 one more time, working row 7 of Diamond Pattern on 37 sts.

Note In order to complete last diamond, work st 7 of Diamond Pattern with Yarn C after repeating pattern 6 times.

Rep rows 3–4 one more time.

Row 19: P to wrapped st, p the wrap and st tog, p to end.

Next Row: K all sts.

Short Rows

Row 1 (WS): P72, wrap and turn.

Row 2: Work back the other way, k to end.

Beg Diamond Pattern

Row 3: P3, with Yarn C, *work row 1 of Diamond Pattern on 37 sts, rep pattern 6 times, with Yarn A, p to last 8 sts before wrapped st, wrap and turn.

Row 4: K to 37 sts of Diamond Pattern, work row 2 of Diamond Pattern on 37 sts, rep pattern 6 times, with Yarn A, k3.

Rep rows 3–4 two more times, working Rows 3–6 of Diamond Pattern on 37 sts.

Rep row 3 one more time, working Row 7 of Diamond Pattern on 37 sts.

Note In order to complete the last diamond, work st 7 of Diamond Pattern with Yarn C after repeating pattern 6 times.

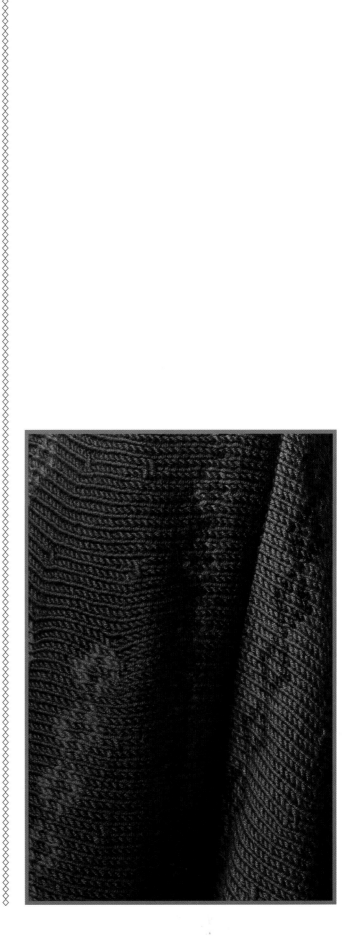

Rep row 2 one more time.

Row 11: P to last 8 sts before wrapped st, wrap and turn.

Row 12: Work back the other way, k to end.

Rep rows 11–12 three more times.

Row 19: *P to wrapped st, p the wrap and st tog, rep from * 9 times, p to end.

Straight Pleat 2
Work in St st for next 6 (8, 10) rows.

Beg Diamond Pattern
Work as indicated for Diamond Pattern of Straight Pleat 1.

Beg with WS row, work in St st for 5 more rows.

Beg Diamond Pattern
Work as indicated for Diamond Pattern of Straight pleat 1.

Beg with WS row, work in St st for 6 (8, 10) more rows.

Godet Pleat 2
Short rows
Row 1 (WS): P8, wrap and turn.

Row 2: Work back the other way, k8.

Row 3: P to wrapped st, p the wrap and st tog, p7, wrap and turn.

Row 4: Work back the other way, k to end.

Rep rows 3–4 seven more times.

Row 19: P to wrapped st, p the wrap and st tog, p to end.

Next Row: K all sts.

Short rows
Row 1 (WS): P72, wrap and turn.

Row 2: Work back the other way, k to end.

Row 3: P to last 8 sts before wrapped st, wrap and turn.

Row 4: Work back the other way, k to end.

Rep rows 3–4 seven more times.

Row 19: *P to wrapped st, p the wrap and st tog, rep from * 9 times, p to end.

Straight Pleat 3
Work in St st for next 31 (35, 39) rows.

Godet Pleat 3
Work same as for Godet Pleat 2.

Straight Pleat 4
Work in St st for next 16 (18, 20) rows.

BO all sts.

BACK

Straight Pleat 1
With crochet hook and Yarn B, loosely ch 90 sts.

With straight needles, pick up and k90 sts, inserting needle in each ch st.

Beg with WS row, work in St st for 16 (18, 20) rows.

Godet Pleat 1
Work same as for Godet Pleat 2 of front.

Straight Pleat 2
Work same as for Straight Pleat 3 of front.

Rep Godet Pleat 1 and Straight Pleat 2 twice.

Rep Godet Pleat 1 one more time.

Straight Pleat 4
Work in St st for next 5 (7, 9) rows.

Beg Diamond Pattern
Beg with RS row and Yarn B, work 2 sts in St st, join Yarn A and *work in Diamond Pattern, rep pattern 14 times over 85 sts (to complete last diamond, work st 7 of Diamond Pattern), cont with Yarn B, work 3 last sts in St st.

Cont as established in pattern illustration for 7 rows.

Note In order to complete the last diamond at row 4, work st 7 of Diamond Pattern with Yarn A after repeating the pattern 14 times.

Beg with WS row, work in St st for 4 more rows.

BO all sts.

FINISHING
Sew side seams.

Waist
With RS of front facing, bottom close to you, using Yarn A and circular needle, beg at right side seam, pick up and k all around skirt top, inserting needle in every other st of skirt top.

Rnds 1–3: K all sts.

Rnd 4 (drawstring holes): K to front center 6 sts, BO 2 sts, k1, BO 2 sts, k to end.

Rnd 5 (drawstring holes): K to front center 6 sts, CO 2 sts, k2, CO 2 sts, k to end.

Rnd 6: K all sts.

Rnd 7: P all sts.

Rnds 8–13: K all sts.

BO all sts.

With WS of skirt facing, bottom close to you, folding waist in half toward the inside of the skirt, sew waist top and skirt top tog with invisible seam.

Bottom border
With RS of front facing, top close to you, using Yarn C and circular needle, pick up and k all across skirt bottom, inserting needle in every other st of skirt bottom.

Rnds 1–3: P all sts.

BO all sts.

Drawstring
With Yarn A and crochet hook, ch 250 sts.

Row 1: Sc in 2 ch from hook and in each of next 248 chs. Fasten off.

With RS of skirt front facing and bottom close to you, using safety pin, insert drawstring into 1st drawstring hole, pull across and out through 2nd drawstring hole at front.

Pompoms (make 2)
Make 1 pompom (page 11) with 2 strands of Yarn A and another with 2 strands of Yarn B.

Sew 1 pompom at either end of drawstring.

This project was knit with

(A) 5 (6, 6) balls of Red Heart Bamboo Wool Yarn, 55% viscose from bamboo/45% wool, medium weight, approx 1.75oz/50g = 80m/87yds per ball, color 3845

(B) 5 (6, 6) balls of Red Heart Bamboo Wool Yarn, 55% viscose from bamboo/45% wool, medium weight, approx 1.75oz/50g = 80m/87yds per ball, color 3650

(C) 1 ball of Red Heart Bamboo Wool Yarn, 55% viscose from bamboo/45% wool, medium weight, approx 1.75oz/50g = 80m/87yds per ball, color 3340

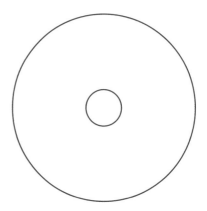

Pompom template

Shapely Short Shorts

Create an incredible fashion statement with these super-young, super-trendy short shorts. Made with eco-friendly yarn that is both cool and comfortable, this unique design features button-up cuffs and a convenient button fly. Worn with unconventional stockings, they won't go unnoticed.

EXPERIENCE LEVEL

▬▬▬▭ Intermediate

SIZES

> 36/38 (40/42, 44/46). Shown in size 36/38.

FINISHED FLAT MEASUREMENTS

> Low waist: 16½"/42cm (18"/46cm, 19½"/49.5cm)

> Hip: 19"/48cm (20½"/52cm, 22"/56cm)

> Length: 15"/38cm (16½"/42cm, 18"/46cm)

> Leg width at bottom: 9½"/24cm

MATERIALS AND TOOLS

> Yarn A: **4** MEDIUM 648 yd/594m of medium weight yarn, nylon/cotton/acrylic/silk, in dark gray

> Yarn B: **4** MEDIUM 216yd/198m of medium weight yarn, nylon/cotton/acrylic/silk, in variegated light gray

> Size 8 (5mm) straight knitting needles OR SIZE TO OBTAIN GAUGE

> Size 8 (5mm) by 24" to 32" circular knitting needles OR SIZE TO OBTAIN GAUGE

> Size E/4 (3.5) crochet hook OR SIZE TO OBTAIN GAUGE

> Three buttons, ¾"/2cm diameter

> Three buttons, 1"/2.5cm diameter

> Scissors

> Yarn needle

> Sewing needle and thread

GAUGE

> In St st, 17 sts and 25 rows to 4"/10cm

Measurements

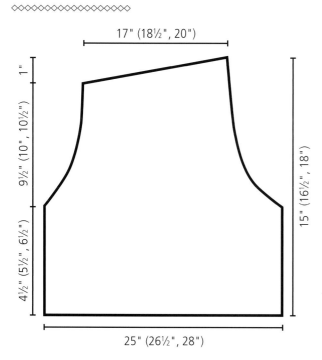

17" (18½", 20")

1"

9½" (10", 10½")

4½" (5½", 6½")

15" (16½", 18")

25" (26½", 28")

Instructions

2-Stitch Wide Left Fold

Each fold consists of 6 sts and 1 row.

With RS of work facing, insert hook from front to back into next st at row indicated.

Sk next 2 sts and insert hook from back to front into next st (3rd st from hook). Insert hook from front to back into next st.

Grab yarn and draw through work.

Draw yarn through all sts and through lp on hook.

Insert hook from front to back into back lp of next st.

Insert hook from front to back into next unused st (4th st from hook).

Grab yarn and draw through work.

Draw yarn through all sts and through lp on hook.

Rep all steps to make required number of folds.

2-Stitch Wide Right Fold

Each fold consists of 6 sts and 1 row.

With RS of work facing, insert hook from front to back into front lp of 5th st from hook at row indicated.

Insert hook from front to back into 1st st of fold (st corresponding to 5th st of fold).

Grab yarn and draw through work.

Draw yarn through all sts and through lp on hook.

Insert hook from front to back into next st, from back to front into 3rd st of fold, and from front to back into 2nd st of fold (sts corresponding to 6th st of fold).

Grab yarn and draw through work.

Draw yarn through all sts and through lp on hook.

Repeat steps to make required number of folds.

LEFT HALF
Left leg
With Yarn A, cast on 108 (114, 120) sts.

Beg at bottom of leg and WS (purl) row, work in St st for 27 (33, 39) rows (end with WS row).

Left bottom
Work next 8 rows, making dec as indicated at beginning of each row for front and back curve, as follows:

Row 1: BO 6 sts in knit (for back curve), k to end—102 (108, 114) sts.

Row 2: BO 3 sts in purl (for front curve), p to end—99 (105, 111) sts.

Row 3: BO 4 sts in knit (for back curve), k to end—95 (101, 107) sts.

Row 4: BO 2 sts in purl (for front curve), p to end—93 (99, 105) sts.

Row 5: BO 2 sts in knit (for back curve), k to end—91 (97, 103) sts.

Row 6: BO 1 st in purl (for front curve), p to end—90 (96, 102) sts.

Row 7: BO 1 st in knit (for back curve), k to end—89 (95, 101) sts.

Row 8: BO 1 st in purl (for front curve), p to end—88 (94, 100) sts.

*Next Row (Dec Row): K1, k2tog, k to last 3 sts, skp, k1.

Beg at WS row, work in St st for 3 more rows.

Rep from * 7 more times—72 (78, 84) sts.

Work in St st for next 20 (24, 28) rows.

Cont and work next 6 rows as follows:

Short rows
Row 1: K18 (k20, k21) sts, wrap and turn.

Row 2 and each even row: Work back the other way, p to end.

Row 3: K to wrapped st, k wrap and st tog, k17 (k19, k20), wrap and turn.

Rep rows 2–3 once more.

Rep row 2 one more time.

Row 7: K all sts.

BO all sts in purl.

RIGHT HALF
Right leg
Follow same instruction as for left leg.

Right bottom
Work next 8 rows, making dec as indicated at beg of each row for front and back curve, as follows:

Row 1: BO 3 sts in knit (for front curve), k to end—105 (111, 117) sts.

Row 2: BO 6 sts in purl (for back curve), p to end—99 (105, 111) sts.

Row 3: BO 2 sts in knit (for front curve), k to end—97 (103, 109) sts.

Row 4: BO 4 sts in purl (for back curve), p to end—93 (99, 105) sts.

Row 5: BO 1 st in knit (for front curve), k to end—92 (98, 104) sts.

Row 6: BO 2 sts in purl (for back curve), p to end—90 (96, 102) sts.

Row 7: BO 1 st in knit (for front curve), k to end—89 (95, 101) sts.

Row 8: BO 1 st in purl (for back curve), p to end—88 (94, 100) sts.

*Next Row (Dec Row): K1, k2tog, k to last 3 sts, skp, k1.

Beg at WS row, work in St st for 3 more rows.

Rep from * 7 more times—72 (78, 84) sts.

For size 40/42 (44/46) only
Work in St st for next 4 (8) rows.

For all sizes
Cut Yarn A.

With Yarn A, CO 7 more sts for fly flap, cont and k to end—79 (85, 91) sts.

Beg at WS row, work in St st for next 19 rows.

Cont and work next 7 rows as follows:

Short rows
Row 1: K all sts.

Row 2: P18 (p20, p21) sts, wrap and turn.

Row 3: Work back the other way, k18 (k20, k21).

Row 4: P to wrapped st, p the wrap and st tog, p17 (p19, p20), wrap and turn.

Rep rows 3–4 twice.

Row 7: K all sts.

BO all sts in purl.

FINISHING
Sew leg seams.
Sew back center and front crotch seam until fly.

Inner fly
With WS of shorts front facing, bottom close to you, using Yarn B and crochet hook, loosely work 9 overlay chs along 1st row of fly flap, beg from left half edge and inserting hook in each st (of 1st nine sts) of this row. Fasten off.

With WS of shorts front facing, bottom close to you, using Yarn A and straight needles, pick up and k9 sts, inserting needle in back lp only of each overlay ch.

*Work in St st for next 4 rows.

Buttonhole Row 1: K4 sts, BO 1 st for buttonhole, k to end.

Buttonhole Row 2: P4, CO 1 st for buttonhole, p to end.

Rep from * 2 more times.

Work in St st for 4 more rows.

BO all sts.

With WS of shorts front facing, bottom close to you, using Yarn A and crochet hook, loosely work overlay chs all around each inner fly buttonhole. Fasten off.

With WS of shorts front facing, bottom to your right, using Yarn B and crochet hook, loosely work 23 overlay chs along right inner fly edge from bottom to top, inserting hook in each row space between 1st and 2nd sts of inner fly. Fasten off.

With WS of shorts front facing, bottom to your right, using Yarn B and crochet hook, loosely work 23 overlay chs along left inner fly edge from bottom to top, inserting hook in each row space between last and one before last sts of inner fly and its corresponding st on left half of shorts. Fasten off.

Waist
With WS of shorts front facing, bottom close to you, using Yarn B and crochet hook, work 9 overlay chs along inner fly top, inserting hook in each last row st of inner fly and its corresponding st on left half of shorts, and then loosely work overlay chs all around shorts top, inserting hook in each last row st of left and right half. Fasten off.

With RS of shorts front facing, bottom close to you, using Yarn A and circular needles, pick up and k all around shorts top, inserting needle in front lp only (from top to bottom at WS) of each overlay ch.

Work in St st for next 3 rows, beg with WS row.

Buttonhole Row 1: K to last 5 sts, BO 2 sts for buttonhole, k to end.

Buttonhole Row 2: P3, CO 2 sts for buttonhole, p to end.

Work in St st for 3 more rows.

BO all sts in purl.

With WS of shorts front facing, bottom to your right, using Yarn B and crochet hook, loosely work 10 overlay chs along left waist edge from bottom to top, inserting hook in each row space between 1st and 2nd sts, then loosely work overlay chs all around waist top, inserting hook in each last row st and 33 overlay chs along right waist edge from top to bottom of fly overlap, inserting hook in each row space between 1st and 2nd sts. Fasten off.

With WS of shorts front facing, bottom close to you, using Yarn B and crochet hook, loosely work overlay chs all around waist buttonhole. Fasten off.

Left/right leg cuff
2 stitch wide folds
With WS of shorts back/front facing, top close to you, using Yarn B and crochet hook, beg at rightmost edge of back/front right/left leg, inserting hook in each 1st row st of left/right leg, loosely work overlay chs all around right/left leg bottom as follows:

Work 4 overlay chs along right/left leg bottom, then make three 2-stitch wide right folds, cont and work overlay chs all around right/left leg bottom to the point corresponding with leftmost fold of back/front right/left leg, make three 2-stitch wide left folds, cont and work 4 overlay chs to end. Fasten off.

Left leg cuff
With RS of shorts back facing, top close to you, using Yarn A and circular needles, beg at rightmost edge of back left leg, CO 7 sts for left cuff overlap, pick up k all around left leg bottom, inserting needle in front lp only (from top to bottom at WS) of each overlay ch.

Work in St st for next 3 rows, beg with WS row.

Buttonhole Row 1: K to last 5 sts, BO 2 sts for buttonhole, k to end.

Buttonhole Row 2: P3, CO 2 sts for buttonhole, p to end.

Work in St st for 3 more rows.

BO all sts in purl.

Right leg cuff

With RS of shorts front facing, top close to you, using Yarn A and circular needles, beg at rightmost edge of front right leg, pick up and k all around right leg bottom, inserting needle in front lp only (from top to bottom at WS) of each overlay ch, cont and CO 7 sts for right cuff overlap.

Work in St st for next 3 rows, beg with WS row.

Buttonhole Row 1: K3, BO 2 sts for buttonhole, k to end.

Buttonhole Row 2: P to last 5sts, CO 2 sts for buttonhole, p to end.

Work in St st for 3 more rows.

BO all sts in purl.

With WS of shorts facing, top close to you, using Yarn B and crochet hook, loosely work overlay chs all around each cuff buttonhole. Fasten off.

With WS of shorts front/back facing, top close to your right/bottom close to you, using Yarn B and crochet hook, loosely work overlay chs all around left/right cuff loose edges, inserting hook in each row space between 1st and 2nd sts/in each 1st row st of cuff overlap, then in each last row st of cuff/in each row space between 1st and 2nd sts, then in each row space between 1st and 2nd sts/in each last row st of cuff and in each 1st row st of cuff overlap/in each row space between 1st and 2nd sts. Fasten off.

Sew bottom of fly overlap and bottom of fly inner flap tog.

Sew buttons on appropriate places: 3 smaller buttons on inner fly, 1 larger button on shorts waist and other 2 larger buttons on leg cuffs.

This project was knit with

(A) 3 (4, 4) ball of Berroco Remix yarn, 30% nylon/27% cotton/24% acrylic/10% silk/9% linen, medium weight, approx 3.5oz/100g = 216yd/198m per ball, color 3967

(B) 1 ball of Berroco Remix yarn, 30% nylon/27% cotton/24% acrylic/10% silk/9% linen, medium weight, approx 3.5oz/100g = 216yd/198m per ball, color 3933

Sassy Spring Skirt

This stylish skirt is knit with bamboo yarns in earthy tones for a beautiful effect, both visually and sensually. It features horizontal tucks of varying lengths, and is knitted in rounds so there aren't any seams. It's lovely on its own or worn as a set with the Sassy Spring Blouse (page 99).

EXPERIENCE LEVEL

■■■□ Intermediate

SIZES

> 36/38 (40/42, 44/46). Shown in size 36/38.

FINISHED FLAT MEASUREMENTS

> Length: 23"/57.5cm (23½"/60cm, 24"/61cm)

> Low waist (maximum): 17"/43cm (18½"/47cm, 20"/50cm)

> Hips: 18½"/47cm (20"/50cm, 21½"/55cm)

MATERIALS AND TOOLS

 > 504yd/456m of bulky weight yarn, bamboo viscose/acrylic/polyester, in beige

> Size 10½ (6.5mm) by 24" to 32" circular knitting needles OR SIZE TO OBTAIN GAUGE

> Size 10½ (6.5mm) straight knitting needles OR SIZE TO OBTAIN GAUGE

> Jute twine, rope, or any other drawstring, 2.7yd/2.5m

> 2 stitch markers

> Stitch holder

> Safety pin

> Scissors

GAUGE

> In St st, 13 sts and 18 rows to 4"/10cm

Measurements

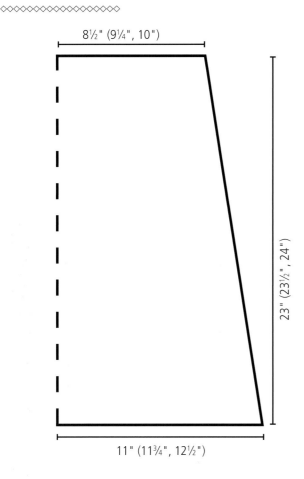

8½" (9¼", 10")

23" (23½", 24")

11" (11¾", 12½")

ELONGATED STITCH PATTERN
Pattern consists of 1 st and 2 rnds.

Rnd 1: *K1, yo twice, rep from * to end of rnd.

Rnd 2: *K1, drop off 2 yarn overs, rep from * to end of rnd.

HORIZONTAL TUCK PATTERN FOR CIRCULAR KNITTING
Pattern consists of 1 st and 4 rnds.

Insert right needle from back of work to front into next st 2 rnds below.

Insert right needle from front of work to back into same st at prev rnd and pull this stitch back (3 rnds below st).

Place pulled stitch onto left needle.

Insert right needle purlwise and k pulled st and next st tog.

Work required number of sts as indicated in pattern instructions.

Instructions

SKIRT

With circular needles, cast on 144 (154, 164) sts.

Beg at bottom of skirt, work in St st (k all sts for circular knitting) for next 3 rnds, marking 1st and 72nd (77th, 82nd) sts [first 72 (77, 82) sts is front and last 72 (77, 82) sts is back of skirt].

Work in Elongated Stitch Pattern for next 2 rnds.

Dec Rnd: Dec 2 sts at front of skirt and 2 sts at back as follows: k1, k2tog, k to last 3 sts of front [2 sts before 72nd (77th, 82nd) marked st], skp, k2, k2tog, k to last 3 sts of back (3 sts before 1st marked st), skp, k1—140 (150, 160) sts.

Work in St st for next 4 rnds, replacing stitch markers and marking 1st and 70th (75th, 80th) sts.

Tuck Rnd 1: *Work next 12 sts in Horizontal Tuck Pattern for side tucks, k46 (k51, k56), work next 12 sts in Horizontal Tuck Pattern for side tucks, rep from * once more.

Work in St st for 1 rnd.

Work in Elongated Stitch Pattern for next 2 rnds.

Rep Dec Rnd once—136 (146, 156) sts.

Work in St st for next 4 rnds, replacing stitch markers and marking 1st and 68th (73rd, 78th) sts.

Tuck Rnd 2: *Work next 8 sts in Horizontal Tuck Pattern for side tucks, k14 (k16, k19), work next 24 (25, 24) sts in Horizontal Tuck Pattern for front/back tucks, k14, work next 8 sts in Horizontal Tuck Pattern for side tucks, rep from * once more.

Work in St st for 1 rnd.

Work in Elongated Stitch Pattern for next 2 rnds.

Rep Dec Rnd once—132 (142, 152) sts.

Work in St st for next 4 rnds, replacing stitch markers and marking 1st and 66th (71st, 76th) sts.

Tuck Rnd 3: *Work next 10 sts in Horizontal Tuck Pattern for side tucks, k46 (k51, k56), work next 10 sts in Horizontal Tuck Pattern for side tucks, rep from * once more.

Work in St st for 1 rnd.

Work in Elongated Stitch Pattern for next 2 rnds.

Rep Dec Rnd once—128 (138, 148) sts.

Work in St st for next 4 rnds, replacing stitch markers and marking 1st and 64th (69th, 74th) sts.

Tuck Rnd 4: *Work next 8 sts in Horizontal Tuck Pattern for side tucks, k14 (k16, k19), work next 20 (21, 20) sts in Horizontal Tuck Pattern for front/back tucks, k14 (k16, k19), work next 8 sts in Horizontal Tuck Pattern for side tucks, rep from * once more.

Work in St st for next 6 rnds.

Rep Dec Rnd once—124 (134, 144) sts.

Work in St st for next 4 rnds, replacing stitch markers and marking 1st and 62nd (67th, 72nd) sts.

Tuck Rnd 5: *Work next 9 sts in Horizontal Tuck Pattern for side tucks, k13 (k15, k18), work next 18 (19, 18) sts in Horizontal Tuck Pattern for front/back tucks, k13 (k15, k18), work next 9 sts in Horizontal Tuck Pattern for side tucks, rep from * once more.

Work in St st for next 6 rnds.

Rep Dec Rnd once—120 (130, 140) sts.

Work in St st for next 4 rnds, replacing stitch markers and marking 1st and 60th (65th, 70th) sts.

Tuck Rnd 6: *Work next 10 sts in Horizontal Tuck Pattern for side tucks, k40 (k45, k50), work next 10 sts in Horizontal Tuck Pattern for side tucks, rep from * once more.

Work in St st for next 6 rnds.

Rep Dec Rnd once—116 (126, 136) sts.

Work in St st for next 4 rnds, replacing stitch markers and marking 1st and 58th (63rd, 68th) sts.

Tuck Rnd 7: *Work next 9 sts in Horizontal Tuck Pattern for side tucks, k40 (k45, k50), work next 9 sts in Horizontal Tuck Pattern for side tucks, rep from * once more.

Work in St st for next 6 rnds.

Rep Dec Rnd once—112 (122, 132) sts.

Work in St st for next 4 rnds, replacing stitch markers and marking 1st and 56th (61st, 66th) sts.

Tuck Rnd 8: *Work next 8 sts in Horizontal Tuck Pattern for side tucks, k40 (k45, k50), work next 8 sts in Horizontal Tuck Pattern for side tucks, rep from * once more.

Work in St st for next 6 rnds.

Rep Dec Rnd once—108 (118, 128) sts.

Work in St st for next 2 (4, 6) rnds, replacing stitch markers and marking 1st and 54th (59th, 64th) sts.

Leave all sts on circular needles. Cut yarn.

Drawstring casings
With RS of skirt facing, bottom close to you and straight needles, pick up and k34 (39, 44) sts, beginning 17 sts before 1st stitch marker and inserting needle through sts two rows back from knitting.

Work in St st for 3 rows, beg at purl row. Cut yarn.

Transfer all sts of drawstring casing onto stitch holder.

With RS of skirt facing, bottom close to you and straight needles, pick up and k34 (39, 44) sts, beg 16 sts before 2nd stitch marker and inserting needle through sts two rows back from knitting.

Work in St st for 3 rows, beg at purl row. Cut yarn.

WAIST

Join yarn and cont to work in rnds, knitting tog each picked up st with corresponding st of skirt as follows: *k34 (39, 44) sts, inserting needle into the picked up stitch and corresponding st of skirt, k20, rep from * once more.

Work in St st for next 10 rnds.

BO all sts.

FINISHING

With RS of skirt front facing and bottom close to you, using safety pin, insert drawstring into 1st drawstring casing, pull through to back of skirt, insert into 2nd drawstring casing, pull through to front again.

Make an overhand knot at each end of the rope. Trim ends, leaving a 1"/2.5cm tail and fray.

This project was knit with

8 (9, 10) balls of Bernat Bamboo Yarn, 86% bamboo viscose/12% acrylic/2% polyester, bulky weight, 2.10/60g = 63yd/57m per ball, color 92011

Sassy Spring Blouse

This pretty blouse, featuring horizontal tucks of varying lengths, is made with bamboo yarn that is lovely to touch. It's easy to make and has a wonderfully professional look, thanks to the fact that it doesn't have any seams. For a fabulous set, wear it with the Sassy Spring Skirt (page 90).

EXPERIENCE LEVEL

■■■□ Intermediate

SIZES

> 36 (38/40, 42/44). Shown in size 36.

FINISHED FLAT MEASUREMENTS

> Chest at underarms: 17"/43cm (18"/46cm, 19½"/49.5cm)

> Length: 23½"/60cm (24½"/62cm, 25½"/65cm)

> Upper arms: 8"/20cm (8½"/21.5cm, 9"/23cm)

MATERIALS AND TOOLS

> 378yd/342m of bulky weight yarn, bamboo viscose/acrylic/polyester, in off-white

> Size 10½ (6.5mm) by 24" to 32" circular knitting needles OR SIZE TO OBTAIN GAUGE

> Size H/7 (5mm) crochet hook

> 5 stitch markers

> Stitch holder

> Scissors

GAUGE

> In St st, 13 sts and 18 rows to 4"/10cm

Measurements

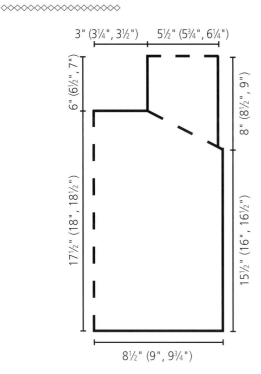

3" (3¼", 3½")   5½" (5¾", 6¼")

6" (6½", 7")

8" (8½", 9")

17½" (18", 18½")

15½" (16", 16½")

8½" (9", 9¾")

ELONGATED STITCH PATTERN

Pattern consists of 1 st and 2 rnds.

Rnd 1: *K1, yo twice, rep from * to end of rnd.

Rnd 2: *K1, drop off 2 yarn overs, rep from * to end of rnd.

HORIZONTAL TUCK PATTERN FOR CIRCULAR KNITTING

Pattern consists of 1 st and 4 rnds.

Insert right needle from back of work to front into next st 2 rnds below.

Insert right needle from front of work to back into same st at prev rnd and pull this stitch back (3 rnds below st).

Place pulled stitch onto left needle.

Insert right needle purlwise and k pulled st and next st tog.

Work required number of sts as indicated in pattern instructions.

Instructions

NECK OPENING

With crochet hook, loosely ch 120 (128, 136) sts. Join with sl st in 1st ch to form a ring.

With circular needles, pick up and k120 (128, 136) sts, inserting needle in each ch st.

FRONT, BACK AND SLEEVES (FROM NECK OPENING TO UNDERARMS)

Beg at top of blouse, work in St st (k all sts for circular knitting) for 1 rnd, marking 1st st, 17th (18th, 19th) st, 44th (47th, 50th) st, 77th (82nd, 87th) st, and 104th (111th, 118th) st for raglan armhole shaping [first 16 (17, 18) sts are half of blouse back, next 26 (28, 30) sts are left sleeve, next 32 (34, 36) sts are blouse front, next 26 (28, 30) sts are right sleeve, last 16 (17, 18) sts are other half of back].

Inc Rnd: Work in St st, inc 1 st before and after each marked st except 1st st of rnd—128 (136, 144) sts.

Work in St st for 1 rnd.

Rep Inc Rnd once—136 (144, 152) sts.

Work in Elongated Stitch Pattern for next 2 rnds.

Rep Inc Rnd once—144 (152, 160) sts.

Work in St st for 1 rnd.

Rep Inc Rnd once—152 (160, 168) sts.

Work in St st for 1 rnd.

Rep Inc Rnd once—160 (168, 176) sts.

Tuck Rnd 1: *Work next 5 sts in Horizontal Tuck Pattern for sleeve tucks, k25 (k27, k29), work next 20 sts in Horizontal Tuck Pattern for front/back tucks, k25 (k27, k29), work next 5 sts in Horizontal Tuck Pattern for sleeve tucks, rep from * once more.

Rep Inc Rnd once—168 (176, 184) sts.

Work in Elongated Stitch Pattern for next 2 rnds.

Rep Inc Rnd once—176 (184, 192) sts.

Work in St st for 1 rnd.

Rep Inc Rnd once—184 (192, 200) sts.

Work in St st for 1 rnd.

Rep Inc Rnd once—192 (200, 208) sts.

Tuck Rnd 2: *Work next 7 sts in Horizontal Tuck Pattern for sleeve tucks, k29 (k31, k33), work next 24 sts in Horizontal Tuck Pattern for front/back tucks, k29, work next 7 sts in Horizontal Tuck Pattern for sleeve tucks, rep from * once more.

Rep Inc Rnd once—200 (208, 216) sts.

Work in St st for 1 rnd.

Next Rnd: *BO 26 (27, 28) sts for sleeve, k48 (k50, k52) for front/back, BO next 26 (27, 28) sts for sleeve, rep from * once more. Cut yarn.

FRONT AND BACK (FROM UNDERARMS TO BOTTOM)

Next Rnd: *K48 (k50, k52) for front/back, pick up and k1, inserting needle into 1st bound-off st of sleeve, pick up and k1, inserting needle into last bound-off st of sleeve, rep from * once more—100 (104, 108) sts.

Work in St st for 11 rnds.

Tuck Rnd 3: *K13 (k14, k15), work next 24 sts in Horizontal Tuck Pattern for front/back tucks, k13 (k14, k15), rep from * once more.

Work in St st for 1 rnd.

Work in Elongated Stitch Pattern for next 2 rnds.

Work in St st for 5 rnds.

Tuck Rnd 4: *K16 (k17, k18), work next 18 sts in Horizontal Tuck Pattern for front/back tucks, k16 (k17, k18), rep from * once more.

Work in St st for 10 rnds.

Tuck Rnd 5: *K17 (k18, k19), work next 16 sts in Horizontal Tuck Pattern for front/back tucks, k17 (k18, k19), rep from * once more.

Work in St st for 20 rnds.

Tuck Rnd 6: *Work next 10 sts in Horizontal Tuck Pattern for side tucks, k30 (k32, k34), work next 10 sts in Horizontal Tuck Pattern for side tucks, rep from * once more.

Work in St st for 6 (8, 10) rnds.

BO all sts.

This project was knit with

6 (7, 8) balls of Bernat Bamboo Yarn, 86% bamboo viscose/12% acrylic/2% polyester, bulky weight, 2.10/60g = 63yd/57m per ball, color 92008

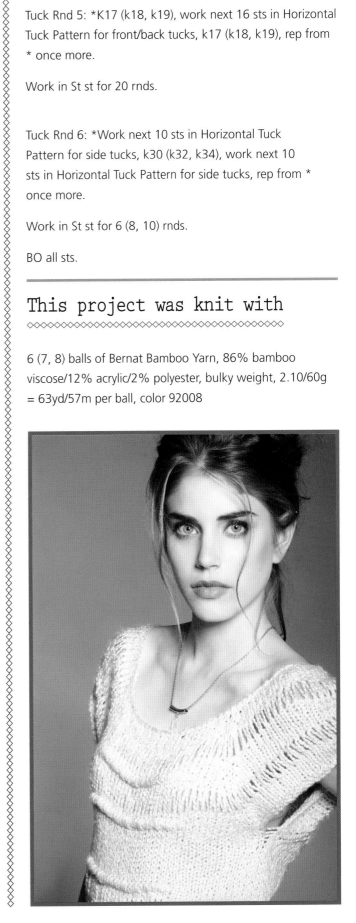

Zigzag Mini Dress

With richly-colored zigzags on an earthy-colored background, this stylish mini dress is a definite showstopper. Striking patterns are created with both yarn color and knit patterns for a doubly distinctive appearance. The ribbed low waist makes it figure-flattering too.

EXPERIENCE LEVEL

■■■☐ Intermediate

SIZES

> 36 (38/40, 42/44). Shown in size 36.

FINISHED FLAT MEASUREMENTS

> Chest at underarms: 16½"/42cm (18"/46cm, 19¾"/50cm)

> Length: 39½"/100cm (39½"/100cm, 40"/102cm)

> Upper arms: 7½"/19cm (7½"/19cm, 8"/20cm)

MATERIALS AND TOOLS

> Yarn A: **MEDIUM 4** 648 yd/594m of medium weight yarn, nylon/cotton/acrylic/silk, in light yellow

> Yarn B: **MEDIUM 4** 216yd/198m of medium weight yarn, nylon/cotton/acrylic/silk, in variegated gray

> Yarn C: **MEDIUM 4** 216yd/198m of medium weight yarn, nylon/cotton/acrylic/silk, in variegated brown and white

> Yarn D: **MEDIUM 4** 216yd/198m of medium weight yarn, nylon/cotton/acrylic/silk, in bright orange

> Size 8 (5mm) by 24" to 32" circular knitting needles OR SIZE TO OBTAIN GAUGE

> Stitch holder

> Scissors

> Yarn needle

GAUGE

> In St st, 17 sts and 25 rows to 4"/10cm

> In Zigzag Pattern, 20 sts and 25 rows to 4"/10cm

Measurements

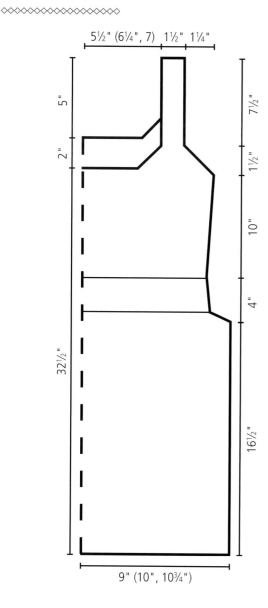

ZIGZAG PATTERN FOR CIRCULAR KNITTING

Pattern consists of 20 (22, 24) sts and 2 rnds.

Rnd 1: *K2tog, k7 (k8, k9), inc 1 from each of next 2 sts, k7 (k8, k9), skp, rep from * required number of times

Rnd 2: K all sts.

Instructions

DRESS BODY

With circular needles and Yarn A, cast on 180 (198, 216) sts.

Beg at bottom of skirt, work in St st (k all sts for circular knitting) for next 2 rnds.

Beg Zigzag Pattern

Rnd 1: Work rnd 1 of Zigzag Pattern, rep from * 9 times.

Rnd 2: Work rnd 2 of Zigzag Pattern.

Rep rnds 1–2 four times. Cut Yarn A.

Join Yarn B, rep rnds 1–2 once. Cut Yarn B.

Join Yarn C, rep rnds 1–2 once. Cut Yarn C.

Join Yarn A, rep rnds 1–2 once. Cut Yarn A.

Join Yarn D, rep rnds 1–2 once. Cut Yarn D.

Join Yarn B, rep rnds 1–2 once. Cut Yarn B.

Join Yarn D, rep rnds 1–2 once. Cut Yarn D.

Join Yarn A, rep rnds 1–2 twice. Cut Yarn A.

Join Yarn C, rep rnds 1–2 twice. Cut Yarn C.

Join Yarn A, rep rnds 1–2 once. Cut Yarn A.

Join Yarn C, rep rnds 1–2 once. Cut Yarn C.

Join Yarn A, rep rnds 1–2 once. Cut Yarn A.

Join Yarn B, rep rnds 1–2 twice. Cut Yarn B.

Join Yarn C, rep rnds 1–2 twice. Cut Yarn C.

Join Yarn A, rep rnds 1–2 once. Cut Yarn A.

Join Yarn D, rep rnds 1–2 twice. Cut Yarn D.

Join Yarn B, rep rnds 1–2 twice. Cut Yarn B.

Join Yarn A, rep rnds 1–2 twice. Cut Yarn A.

Join Yarn C, rep rnds 1–2 twice. Cut Yarn C.

Join Yarn A, rep rnds 1–2 once. Cut Yarn A.

Join Yarn C, rep rnds 1–2 once. Cut Yarn C.

Join Yarn A, rep rnds 1–2 four times.

Work in St st for 16 more rnds.

Dec Rnd: *K2tog, k4, skp, k1, rep from* 19 (21, 23) more times—140 (154, 168) sts.

For sizes 36 (42/44) only
Work in (k2, p2) rib pattern all around for next 24 rnds.

For size 38/40 only
Work for next 24 rows as follows:

Work in (k2, p2) rib pattern 9 times, k3, work in (k2, p2) rib pattern 19 times, k3, work in (k2, p2) rib pattern 9 more times.

For all sizes
Work in St st for 1 more rnd.

Beg Zigzag Pattern
Rnd 1: Work rnd 1 of Zigzag Pattern, rep from * 7 times.

Rnd 2: Work rnd 2 of Zigzag Pattern.

Rep rnds 1–2 twice. Cut Yarn A.

Join Yarn B, rep rnds 1–2 twice. Cut Yarn B.

Join Yarn C, rep rnds 1–2 twice. Cut Yarn C.

Join Yarn A, rep rnds 1–2 once. Cut Yarn A.

Join Yarn C, rep rnds 1–2 once. Cut Yarn C.

Join Yarn A, rep rnds 1–2 twice.

Work in St st for 40 more rnds.

FRONT TOP
Transfer last 35 (38, 42) sts and first 35 (39, 42) sts of last rnd onto stitch holder (beg of rnd is center of back). Rem 70 (77, 84) sts are front of dress.

Armhole shaping

Row 1: K1, k2tog, k to last 3 sts, skp, k1.

Row 2: K1, p to last st, k1.

Rep rows 1–2 three more times—62 (69, 76) sts.

STRAPS

Row 1: For left strap, work in (k2, p2) rib pattern twice, k3, skp, k1, BO next 34 (41, 48) sts for front neckline, work k1, k2tog, k3, (p2, k2) rib twice for right strap. Leave rem 13 sts on stitch holder for left strap.

Right strap

Row 2 and each even row: Always k 1st and last edge sts then k the knits and p the purls.

Row 3: K1, k2tog, k2, (p2, k2) rib twice.

Row 5: K1, k2tog, k1, (p2, k2) rib twice.

Row 7: K1, k2tog, (p2, k2) rib twice—10 sts.

Row 9: K2, (p2, k2) rib twice.

Row 10: Rep row 2.

Rep rows 9–10 nine (nine, eleven) more times.

BO all sts.

Left strap

Work to correspond to right strap, reversing shaping.

Work skp instead of k2tog.

BACK
Armhole shaping

Row 1: K1, k2tog, k to last 3 sts, skp, k1.

Row 2: K1, p to last st, k1.

Rep rows 1–2 three more times— 62 (69, 76) sts.

Work in St st for 10 more rows, always k 1st and last edge sts.

Straps

Work row 1 of front straps.

Left strap

Work rows 2–10 of front right strap.

Rep rows 9–10 five (five, six) times.

BO all sts.

Right strap

Work rows 2–10 of front left strap.

Rep rows 9–10 five (five, six) times.

BO all sts.

FINISHING

Sew strap seams.

This project was knit with

(A) 3 (4, 5) balls of Berroco Remix yarn, 30% nylon/27% cotton/24% acrylic/10% silk/9% linen, medium weight, approx 3.5oz/100g = 216yd/198m per ball, color 3922

(B) 1 ball of Berroco Remix yarn, 30% nylon/27% cotton/24% acrylic/10% silk/9% linen, medium weight, approx 3.5oz/100g = 216yd/198m per ball, color 3933

(C) 1 ball of Berroco Remix yarn, 30% nylon/27% cotton/24% acrylic/10% silk/9% linen, medium weight, approx 3.5oz/100g = 216yd/198m per ball, color 3912

(D) 1 ball of Berroco Remix yarn, 30% nylon/27% cotton/24% acrylic/10% silk/9% linen, medium weight, approx 3.5oz/100g = 216yd/198m per ball, color 3924

Single Strap Beach Tunic

Brighten up a day at the beach with this sexy asymmetrical tunic. The single strap is decorated with a crocheted wild flower, while the rest of the tunic is slim and sleek. Gorgeous for the beach or a hot day in the city!

EXPERIENCE LEVEL

■■■□ Intermediate

SIZES

> 36/38 (40/42). Shown in size 36/38.

FINISHED FLAT MEASUREMENTS

> Chest at underarms: 16"/40cm (18"/46cm)

> Length: Longer side: 38"/96.5cm (40½"/103cm)

> Shorter side: 32"/81cm (34½"/88cm)

> Upper arms: 7½"/19cm

MATERIALS AND TOOLS

> Yarn A: **MEDIUM 4** 555yd/507m of medium worsted weight yarn, recycled cotton/acrylic/other fibers, in variegated white and green

> Yarn B: **MEDIUM 4** 216yd/198m of medium worsted weight yarn, nylon/cotton/acrylic/silk/linen, in variegated yellow and white

> Size 11 (8mm) straight knitting needles OR SIZE TO OBTAIN GAUGE

> Brooch pinback with 2 sewing holes, 1¼"/3cm long

> Scissors

> Yarn needle

> Sewing needle and thread

GAUGE

> In St st, 13 sts and 15 rows to 4"/10cm

Measurements

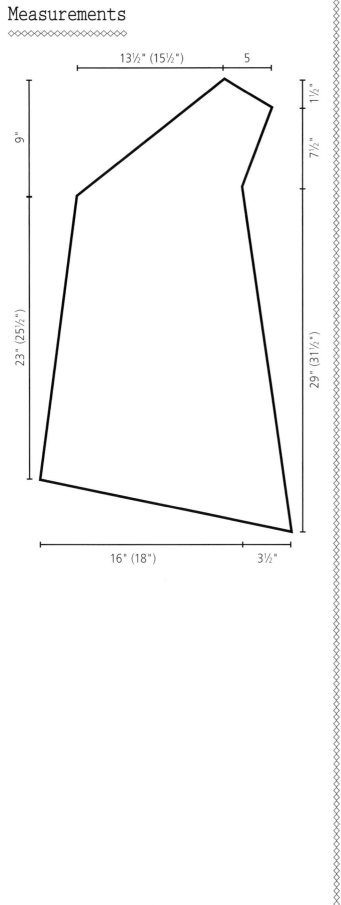

13½" (15½") 5

9"

1½"

7½"

23" (25½")

29" (31½")

16" (18") 3½"

Instructions

FRONT

With Yarn A, cast on 64 (70) sts.

Row 1(WS): P all sts.

Short rows

Row 2: K8, wrap and turn.

Row 3: Work back the other way, p8.

Row 4: K to wrapped st, k the wrap and st tog, k5 (k6), wrap and turn.

Row 5: Work back the other way, p to end.

Rep rows 4–5 seven more times.

Next Row: K to wrapped st, k the wrap and st tog, k7.

Rep row 5.

Work in St st for next 80 (90) rows, dec 1 st at each side (Dec Row) of 1st, 15th (17th) and then each 16th (18th) row 4 times, as follows:

Dec Row: K1, k2tog, k to last 3 sts, skp, k 1—52 (58) sts.

Left armhole and neckline shaping

Work next 28 rows as follows:

Short rows

Row 1: K1, inc1, k to last 5 (6) sts, wrap and turn.

Row 2 and each even row: Work back the other way, p to end.

Row 3: K1, inc1, k to last 5 sts before wrapped st, wrap and turn.

Row 5: K to last 4 (5) sts before wrapped st, wrap and turn.

Row 7: K1, inc1, k to last 4 sts before wrapped st, wrap and turn.

Row 9: K to last 3 (4) sts before wrapped st, wrap and turn.

Row 11: K1, inc1, k to last 3 (4) sts before wrapped st, wrap and turn.

Row 13: K to last 2 (3) sts before wrapped st, wrap and turn.

Row 15: K1, inc1, k to last 2 (3) sts before wrapped st, wrap and turn.

Row 16: Work back the other way, p to end.

Rep rows 13–16 three more times—60 (66) sts.

Left shoulder and neckline shaping
Cont and work next 6 rows as follows:

Short rows
Row 1: BO 6 sts for left shoulder, k to last 2 sts before wrapped st, wrap and turn.

Row 2 and each even row: Work back the other way, p to end.

Row 3: BO 5 sts for left shoulder, k to last 2 sts before wrapped st, wrap and turn.

Row 5: BO 5 sts for left shoulder, k to end, knitting each wrap and st tog.

BO all rem 44 (50) sts in purl.

BACK
With Yarn A, cast on 64 (70) sts.

Row 1(RS): K all sts.

Short rows
Row 2: P8, wrap and turn.

Row 3: Work back the other way, k8.

Row 4: P to wrapped st, p the wrap and st tog, p5, wrap and turn.

Row 5: Work back the other way, k to end.

Rep rows 4–5 seven more times.

Next Row: P to wrapped st, p the wrap and st tog, p7.

Rep row 5.

Work in St st for next 80 (90) rows (beg at WS), dec 1 st at each side (Dec Row) of 2nd, 16th, (18th) and then each 16th (18th) row 4 times, as follows:

Dec Row: K1, k2tog, k to last 3 sts, skp, k1—52 (58) sts.

Left armhole and neckline shaping
Work next 28 rows as follows:

Short rows
Row 1: P to last 5 (6) sts, wrap and turn.

Row 2 and each even row: Work back the other way, k to last 2 sts, inc1, k1.

Row 3: P to last 5 sts before wrapped st, wrap and turn.

Row 5: P to last 4 (5) sts before wrapped st, wrap and turn.

Row 7: P to last 4 sts before wrapped st, wrap and turn.

Row 9: P to last 3 (4) sts before wrapped st, wrap and turn.

Row 11: P to last 3 (4) sts before wrapped st, wrap and turn.

Row 13: P to last 2 (3) sts before wrapped st, wrap and turn.

Row 15: P to last 2 (3) sts before wrapped st, wrap and turn.

Row 16: Work back the other way, k to last 2 sts, inc1, k1.

Rep rows 13–16 four times—60 (66) sts.

Left shoulder and neckline shaping
Cont and work next 6 rows as follows:

Short rows
Row 1: BO 6 sts in purl for left shoulder, p to last 2 sts before wrapped st, wrap and turn.

Row 2 and each even row: Work back the other way, k to end.

Row 3: BO 5 sts in purl for left shoulder, p to last 2 sts before wrapped st, wrap and turn.

Row 5: BO 5 sts in purl for left shoulder, p to end, knitting each wrap and st tog.

BO all rem 44 (50) sts in knit.

Crocheted string (optional)
With Yarn B and crochet hook, ch 200 sts.

Row 1: Sl st in 1st ch from hook and in each of next 199 chs. Fasten off.

CROCHETED FLOWER (OPTIONAL)
Flower center
With Yarn B and crochet hook, ch 6, join with sl st in 1st ch to form a ring.

Rnd 1: Ch 1, 12 sc in ring. Join with sl st 1st sc.

Rnd 2: Ch 1, inserting hook in back lp only, sc in same sc as joining, 2 sc in next sc, *sc in next sc, 2 sc in next sc. Rep from * 5 times. Join with sl st 1st sc—18 sc

Rnd 3: Ch 1, inserting hook in back lp only, sc in same sc as joining and in next sc, 2 sc in next sc, *sc in each of next 2 sc, 2 sc in next sc. Rep from * 5 times. Join with sl st 1st sc—24 sc.

Stamens
With RS of flower center facing and Yarn A, insert hook in each unused lp of rnd 1 of flower center to make 12 stamens as follows:

1st stamen
Row 1: Insert hook, from top to bottom (pointing to center) in 12th unused lp of rnd 1 of flower center, sl st. Ch 8.

Row 2: Sl st into 2nd ch from hook and in each of next 6 chs, sl st in 12th unused lp of rnd 1 of flower center.

Note Don't cut yarn after finishing each stamen, simply continue working in the round, beginning each stamen in each next unused loop of round 1 of the flower center.

2nd (3rd, 6th) stamen
Row 1: Cont and sl st in 11th (10th, 7th) unused lp of rnd 1 of flower center, ch 9.

Row 2: Sl st into 2nd ch from hook and in each of next 7 chs, sl st in 11th (10th, 7th) unused lp of rnd 1 of flower center.

4th (5th, 8th, 9th) stamen
Row 1: Cont and sl st in 9th (8th, 5th, 4th) unused lp of rnd 1 of flower center, ch 10.

Row 2: Sl st into 2nd ch from hook and in each of next 8 chs, sl st in 9th (8th, 5th, 4th) unused lp of rnd 1 of flower center.

7th (12th) stamen
Row 1: Cont and sl st in 6th (1st) unused lp of rnd 1 of flower center, ch 12.

Row 2: Sl st into 2nd ch from hook and in each of next 10 chs, sl st in 6th (1st) unused lp of rnd 1 of flower center.

10th stamen
Row 1: Cont and sl st in 3rd unused lp of rnd 1 of flower center, ch 18.

Row 2: Sl st into 2nd ch from hook and in each of next 16 chs, sl st in 3rd unused lp of rnd 1 of flower center.

11th stamen
Row 1: Cont and sl st in 3rd unused lp of rnd 1 of flower center, ch 16.

Row 2: Sl st into 2nd ch from hook and in each of next 14 chs, sl st in 2nd unused lp of rnd 1 of flower center.

Fasten off.

PETALS
With RS of flower center facing and Yarn B, inserting hook in each unused lp of rnd 2 of flower center make 16 petals as follows:

1st petal
Row 1: Insert hook, from top to bottom (pointing to center) in 16th unused lp of rnd 2 of flower center, sl st. Ch 12.

Row 2: Sl st into 2nd ch from hook and in each of next 10 chs, sl st in 16th unused lp of rnd 2 of flower center.

Note Don't cut yarn after finishing each petal, simply continue working in the round, beginning each petal in each next unused lp of round 2 of flower center.

2nd (3rd, 4th, 5th, 8th, 9th) petal
Row 1: Cont and sl st in 15th (14th, 13th, 12th, 9th, 8th) unused lp of rnd 2 of flower center, ch 14.

Row 2: Sl st into 2nd ch from hook and in each of next 12 chs, sl st in 15th (14th, 13th, 12th, 9th, 8th) unused lp of rnd 2 of flower center.

6th (7th, 10th, 11th, 12th) petal
Row 1: Cont and sl st in 11th (10th, 7th, 6th, 5th) unused lp of flower center, ch 16.

Row 2: Sl st into 2nd ch from hook and in each of next 14 chs, sl st in 11th (10th, 7th, 6th, 5th) unused lp of rnd 2 of flower center.

13th petal
Row 1: Cont and sl st in 4th unused lp of rnd 2 of flower center, ch 18.

Row 2: Sl st into 2nd ch from hook and in each of next 16 chs, sl st in 4th unused lp of rnd 2 of flower center.

14th petal
Row 1: Cont and sl st in 3rd unused lp of rnd 2 of flower center, ch 20.

Row 2: Sl st into 2nd ch from hook and in each of next 18 chs, sl st in 3rd unused lp of rnd 2 of flower center.

15th petal

Row 1: Cont and sl st in 2nd unused lp of rnd 2 of flower center, ch 40.

Row 2: Sl st into 2nd ch from hook and in each of next 38 chs, sl st in 2nd unused lp of rnd 2 of flower center.

16th petal

Row 1: Cont and sl st in 1st unused lp of rnd 2 of flower center, ch 64.

Row 2: Sl st into 2nd ch from hook and in each of next 62 chs, sl st in 1st unused lp of rnd 2 of flower center.

Fasten off.

FINISHING (OPTIONAL)

Sew shoulder seam.

Attach center of crocheted string to left (or right) side of low tunic waist by sewing tog with invisible seam.

Sew brooch pinback to crocheted flower.

This project was knit with

(A) 3 balls of Lion Recycled Cotton Yarn, 72% recycled cotton/24% acrylic/2% other fibers, medium worsted weight, approx 3.5oz/100g = 185yd/169m per ball, color 482-130

(B) 1 ball of Berroco Remix yarn, 30% nylon/27% cotton/24% acrylic/10% silk/9% linen, medium worsted weight, approx 3.5oz/100g = 216yd/198m per ball, color 3922

Unconventional Oxford Vest

This bold vest is a modern twist on a traditional style. It features bright orange cotton yarn, knit in a loose, comfortable net pattern. Made with bright colors and easy-to-care-for yarn, it's ideal for wearing both on and off campus!

EXPERIENCE LEVEL

 Intermediate

SIZES

> 36 (38/40, 42/44). Shown in size 36.

FINISHED FLAT MEASUREMENTS

> Chest at underarms: 17"/43cm (18½"/47cm, 20"/50cm)

> Length: 21"/53cm (22¾"/58cm, 23½"/60cm)

> Upper arms: 7"/18cm (8¼"/21cm, 9"/23cm)

MATERIALS AND TOOLS

> Yarn A: **MEDIUM 4** 725yd/660m of medium weight yarn, recycled cotton/acrylic, in variegated red, yellow and green

> Yarn B: **MEDIUM 4** 145m/132yds of medium weight yarn, recycled cotton/acrylic, in variegated red, yellow, in denim blue

> Yarn C: **MEDIUM 4** 145m/132yds of medium weight yarn, recycled cotton/acrylic, in variegated red, yellow, in bright orange

> Yarn D: **MEDIUM 4** 145m/132yds of medium weight yarn, recycled cotton/acrylic, in variegated red, yellow, in light green

> Size 4 (3.5mm) straight knitting needles OR SIZE TO OBTAIN GAUGE

> Size 4 (3.5mm) by 24" to 32" circular knitting needles OR SIZE TO OBTAIN GAUGE

> Stitch holder

GAUGE

> With Yarn A in Net Pattern, 20 sts and 26 rows to 4"/10cm

> With Yarn B in rib pattern, 20 sts and 26 rows to 4"/10cm

Measurements

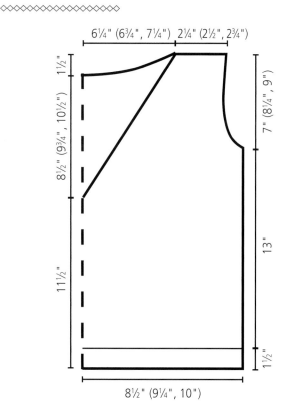

NET PATTERN

Pattern consists of 4 sts and 4 rows.

Row 1: *K1, yo, double left-slanting decrease, yo, rep from * required number of times.

Row 2: P all sts.

Row 3: **Double right-slanting decrease, yo, k1, yo, rep from ** required number of times.

Row 4: Rep row 2.

Instructions

FRONT

With Yarn B and straight needles, cast on 84 (92, 100) sts.

Work in (k2, p2) rib for 4 rows. Cut Yarn B.

Join Yarn C and work in (k2, p2) rib for 2 more rows. Cut Yarn C.

Join Yarn D and work in (k2, p2) rib for 2 more rows. Cut Yarn D.

Join Yarn B and work in (k2, p2) rib for 4 more rows. Cut Yarn B.

Inc Row: Join Yarn A, k1, inc 1, k to last 2 sts, inc 1, k1—86 (94, 102) sts.

Next Row: P all sts.

Beg Net Pattern

Pattern consists of 4 sts and 4 rows.

Work in Net Pattern for next 62 rows as follows:

Row 1: K3, rep from Net Pattern * 20 (22, 24) times, k3.

Row 2: P all sts.

Row 3: K3, rep from Net Pattern ** 20 (22, 24) times, k3.

Row 4: Rep row 2.

Rep rows 1–4 fourteen more times.

Rep rows 1–2 one more time.

V-neck and armhole shaping (left front)

Work each armhole and each side of neck separately as follows:

Row 1: K3, rep from Net Pattern ** 9 (10, 11) times, k1, skp, k1, leave rem 43 (47, 51) sts for right front on a stitch holder.

Row 2 and each even row: P all sts.

Row 3: K3, rep from Net Pattern * 9 (10, 11) times, skp, k1.

Row 5: K3, rep from Net Pattern ** 9 (10, 11) times, k2—41 (45, 49) sts.

Row 7: K3, rep from Net Pattern * 8 (9, 10) times, k3, skp, k1.

Row 9: K3, rep from Net Pattern ** 8 (9, 10) times, k2, skp, k1.

Row 11: K3, rep from Net Pattern * 8 (9, 10) times, k4—39 (43, 47) sts.

Row 13: K3, rep from Net Pattern ** 8 (9, 10) times, k1, skp, k1.

Row 15: K3, rep from Net Pattern * 8 (9, 10) times, skp, k1.

Row 17: BO 3 sts for armhole shaping, k3, rep from Net Pattern ** 7 (8, 9) times, k2—34 (38, 42) sts.

Row 19: BO 2 sts for armhole shaping, k1, rep from Net Pattern * 6 (7, 8) times, k3, skp, k1.

Row 21: BO 1 st for armhole shaping, k4, rep from Net Pattern ** 5 (6, 7) times, k2, skp, k1.

Row 23: BO 1 st for armhole shaping, k3, rep from Net Pattern * 5 (6, 7) times, k4—28 (32, 36) sts.

Row 25: BO 1 st for armhole shaping, k2, rep from Net Pattern ** 5 (6, 7) times, k1, skp, k1.

Row 27: K3, rep from Net Pattern * 5 (6, 7) times, k3—26 (30, 34) sts.

Row 29: K3, rep from Net Pattern ** 5 (6, 7) times, skp, k1.

Row 31: K3, rep from Net Pattern * 4 (5, 6) times, k3, skp, k1.

Row 33: K3, rep from Net Pattern ** 4 (5, 6) times, k5—24 (28, 32) sts.

Row 35: K3, rep from Net Pattern * 4 (5, 6) times, k2, skp, k1.

Row 37: K3, rep from Net Pattern ** 4 (5, 6) times, k1, skp, k1.

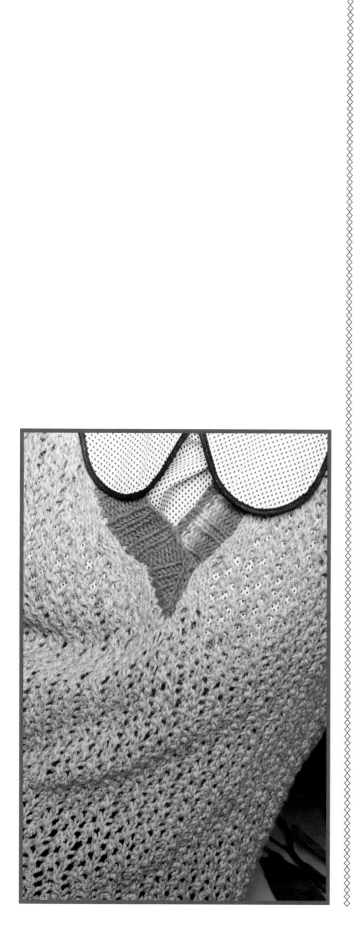

Row 39: K3, rep from Net Pattern * 4 (5, 6) times, k3—22 (26, 30) sts.

Row 41: K3, rep from Net Pattern ** 4 (5, 6) times, skp, k1.

Row 43: K3, rep from Net Pattern * 3 (4, 5) times, k3, skp, k1.

Row 45: K3, rep from Net Pattern ** 3 (4, 5) times, k5—20 (24, 28) sts.

Row 47: K3, rep from Net Pattern * 3 (4, 5) times, k2, skp, k1.

Row 49: K3, rep from Net Pattern ** 3 (4, 5) times, k1, skp, k1.

Row 51: K3, rep from Net Pattern * 3 (4, 5) times, k3—18 (22, 26) sts.

Row 53: K3, rep from Net Pattern ** 3 (4, 5) times, skp, k1.

Row 55: K3, rep from Net Pattern * 2 (3, 4) times, k3, skp, k1.

Row 57: K3, rep from Net Pattern ** 2 (3, 4) times, k5—16 (20, 24) sts.

Row 59: K3, rep from Net Pattern Net Pattern * 2 (3, 4) times, k2, skp, k1.

Row 61: K3, rep from Net Pattern ** 2 (3, 4) times, k1, skp, k1.

Row 63: K3, rep from Net Pattern * 2 (3, 4) times, k3—14 (18, 22) sts.

Row 65: K3, rep from Net Pattern ** 2 (3, 4) times, skp, k1.

Row 67: K3, rep from Net Pattern * 1 (2, 3) times, k3, skp, k1—12 (16, 20) sts.

For sizes 38/40 (42/44) only
Row 69: K3, rep from Net Pattern * 2 (3) times, k5.

Row 71: K3, rep from Net Pattern * 2 (3) times, k2, skp, k1.

Row 73: K3, rep from Net Pattern * 2 (3) times, k1, skp, k1.

Row 75: K3, rep from Net Pattern * 2 (3) times, k3—14 (18) sts.

For size 42/44 only
Row 77: K3, rep from Net Pattern * 2 times, k4, skp, k1.

Row 73: K3, rep from Net Pattern * 2 times, k3, skp, k— 16 sts.

For all sizes
BO all rem 12 (14, 16) sts for left shoulder.

V-neck and armhole shaping (right front)
Work to correspond to left front, reversing shaping.

Work k2tog instead of skp.

Make all BO sts for armhole shaping on rows 18, 20, 22, 24, 26.

Work rows 17, 19, 21, 23, 25 as follows:

Row 17: K2, rep from Net Pattern ** 7 times, k7 (8, 9).

Row 19: K1, k2tog, k3, rep from Net Pattern * 6 (7, 8) times, k4.

Row 21: K1, k2tog, k2, rep from Net Pattern ** 5 (6, 7) times, k6.

Row 23: K4, rep from Net Pattern * 5 (6, 7) times, k5.

Row 25: K1, k2tog, k1, rep from Net Pattern ** 5 times, k4.

Cont as front from row 27, reversing shaping.

BACK
Work same as for front until Net Pattern begins.

Beg Net Pattern
Pattern consists of 4 sts and 4 rows.

Work in Net Pattern for next 78 (82, 86) rows as follows:

Row 1: K3, rep from Net Pattern * 20 (22, 24) times, k3.

Row 2: P all sts.

Row 3: K3, rep from Net Pattern ** 20 (22, 24) times, k3.

Row 4: Rep row 2.

Rep rows 1–4 eighteen more times.

Rep rows 1–2 one more time.

Armhole shaping
Row 1: BO 3 sts for armhole shaping, k3, rep from Net Pattern ** 18 (20, 22) times, k7.

Row 2: BO 3 sts for armhole shaping, p to end—80 (88, 96) sts.

Row 3: BO 2 sts for armhole shaping, k1, rep from Net Pattern * 18 (20, 22) times, k4.

Row 4: BO 2 sts for armhole shaping, p to end—76 (84, 92) sts.

Row 5: BO 1 st for armhole shaping, k4, rep from Net Pattern ** 16 (18, 20) times, k6.

Row 6: BO 1 st for armhole shaping, p to end—74 (82, 90) sts.

Row 7: BO 1 st for armhole shaping, k3, rep from Net Pattern * 16 (18, 20) times, k5.

Row 8: BO 1 st for armhole shaping, p to end—72 (80, 88) sts.

Row 9: BO 1 st for armhole shaping, k2, rep from Net Pattern ** 16 (18, 20) times, k4.

Row 10: BO 1 st for armhole shaping, p to end—70 (78, 86) sts.

Cont to work in Net Pattern for next 30 (38, 42) rows as follows:

Row 1: K3, rep from Net Pattern * 16 (18, 20) times, k3.

Row 2: P all sts.

Row 3: K3, rep from Net Pattern ** 16 (18, 20) times, k3.

Row 4: Rep row 2.

Rep rows 1–4 six more times.

Rep rows 1–2 one more time.

Neck shaping (left back)
Row 1: K3, rep from Net Pattern ** 4 (5, 5) times, k5 (k3, k5), BO next 22 (26, 30) sts for neck opening, k4 (k2, k4), rep from Net Pattern ** 4 (5, 5) times, k3.

Row 2 and each even row: P all sts, leave rem 24 sts for right front on a stitch holder—24 (26, 28) sts.

Row 3: BO 2 sts, k2 (k4, k2), rep from Net Pattern * 4 (4, 5) times, k3.

Row 5: BO 2 sts, k4 (k2, k4), rep from Net Pattern ** 3 (4, 4) times, k3.

Row 7: BO 2 sts, k6 (k4, k2), rep from Net Pattern * 2 (3, 4) times k3.

Row 9: BO 3 sts, k3 (k1, k3), rep from Net Pattern ** 2 (3, 3) times, k3.

Row 11: BO 3 sts, k to end—12 (14, 16) sts.

BO all rem 12 (14, 16) sts for left shoulder.

Neck shaping (right back)
Row 2: P all sts—24 (26, 28) sts.

Row 3: K3, rep from Net Pattern * 4 (5, 5) times, k5 (k3, k5).

Row 4: BO 2 sts, p to end.

Row 5: K3, rep from Net Pattern ** 3(4, 4) times, k7 (k5, k7).

Row 6: BO 2 sts, p to end.

Row 7: K3, rep from Net Pattern * 2 (3, 4) times, k9 (k7, k5).

Row 8: BO 2 sts, p to end.

Row 9: K3, rep from Net Pattern ** 2 (3, 3) times, k7 (k5, k7).

Row 10: BO 3 sts, p to end.

Row 11: K3, rep from Net Pattern * 2 (3, 3), k4 (k2, k4).

Row 12: BO 3 sts, p to end—12 (14, 16) sts.

BO all rem 12 (14, 16) sts for right shoulder.

FINISHING
Sew shoulder and side seams.

Left neck border
With RS of back facing, bottom close to you, using Yarn B and circular needle, beg at center of back neck opening, pick up and k24 (k26, k28) sts across left back neck opening, pick up and k46 (k54, k56) sts down left front v-neck slope—72 (80, 84) sts.

Row 1(WS): P6, work in (k2, p2) rib pattern 16 (18, 19) times, k2.

Row 2: K the knits and p the purls.

Row 3: Rep row 1.

Row 4: P2, work in (k2, p2) rib pattern 16 times (18, 19), k to last 3sts, skp, k1. Cut Yarn B.

Row 5: Join Yarn C, p5, work in (k2, p2) rib pattern 16 (18, 19) times, k2.

Row 6: Rep row 4. Cut Yarn C.

Row 7: Join Yarn D, p4, work in (k2, p2) rib pattern 16 (18, 19) times, k2.

Row 8: Rep row 4. Cut Yarn D.

Row 9: Join Yarn B, p3, work in (k2, p2) rib pattern 16 (18, 19) times, k2.

Row 8: Rep row 4.

BO loosely in rib pattern.

Right neck border
With RS of front facing, bottom close to you, using Yarn B and circular needle, beg at center of front v-neck opening, pick up and k46 (k54, k56) sts up right front v-neck slope,

pick up and k24 (k26, k28) sts across right back neck opening—72 (80, 84) sts.

Work to correspond to left neck border, reversing shaping and using Yarn B only.

Sew front border endings to corresponding v-neck slopes with invisible seams.

Sew back border endings together.

Armhole border

With RS facing, bottom to your right, using Yarn B and circular needle, beg at top of side seam, pick up and k76 (88, 94) sts around each armhole opening.

Join and work in St st for 1 rnd (k all sts).

BO loosely all sts.

This project was knit with

(A) 5 (6, 7) balls of Red Heart Eco-Cotton™ Blend Yarn, 75% recycled cotton/25% acrylic, medium weight, approx 3 oz/85g = 145m/132yds per ball, color 1370

(B) 1 ball of Red Heart Eco-Cotton™ Blend Yarn, 75% recycled cotton/25% acrylic, medium weight, approx 3 oz/85g = 145m/132yds per ball, color 1870

(C) 1 ball of Red Heart Eco-Cotton™ Blend Yarn, 75% recycled cotton/25% acrylic, medium weight, approx 3 oz/85g = 145m/132yds per ball, color 1255

(D) 1 ball of Red Heart Eco-Cotton™ Blend Yarn, 75% recycled cotton/25% acrylic, medium weight, approx 3 oz/85g = 145m/132yds per ball, color 1645

Index

◇◇◇◇◇◇◇

Acknowledgments

◇◇◇◇◇◇◇◇◇◇◇◇◇◇◇◇◇◇◇◇◇

ACCESSORIES
XRAY
www.xray-uv.com
pages 70, 84

HAND BAGS
Eyal Lester
page 48, 58, 70

Maya Shalev
www.mayashalev.com
pages 24, 76, 84, 94, 100

JEWELRY
Ayala Vitkon
www.ayala-v.co.il
pages 36, 42, 48, 52, 64, 84, 94

Efrat Azoz
page 36

Lilla My
www.lilla-my.com
pages 52, 58, 64, 76, 84, 116

SHOES
Shoe Maker
www.shoemaker.co.il
pages 24, 36, 48, 52, 64

UnaUna
www.una-una.com
pages 58, 100

WARDROBE
Eyal Lester
Page 24, 32

Frog
www.frogaspect.com
pages 24, 48, 64, 100

Gusta
www.gusta.co.il
pages 36, 64, 70, 116

Naama Bezalel
www.naamabezalel.com
pages 36, 42, 76, 84, 116